SpringerBriefs in Applied Sciences and Technology

PoliMI SpringerBriefs

W0230494

More information about this subseries at https://link.springer.com/bookseries/11159
http://www.polimi.it

Gabriele Pasqui

Coping with the Pandemic in Fragile Cities

POLITECNICO
MILANO 1863

 Springer

Gabriele Pasqui
Department of Architecture and Urban
Studies (DASTU)
Politecnico di Milano
Milan, Italy

ISSN 2191-530X   ISSN 2191-5318 (electronic)
SpringerBriefs in Applied Sciences and Technology
ISSN 2282-2577   ISSN 2282-2585 (electronic)
PoliMI SpringerBriefs
ISBN 978-3-030-93978-6   ISBN 978-3-030-93979-3 (eBook)
https://doi.org/10.1007/978-3-030-93979-3

This Springer imprint is published by the registered company Springer Nature Switzerland AG
The registered company address is: Gewerbestrasse 11, 6330 Cham, Switzerland

To Valentina

Introduction

Abstract This chapter introduces the book by explaining its conceptual framework and the conditions of its production during the first year of COVID-19 pandemic. The chapter underlines the three main perspectives of the book: the centrality of socio-spatial dimension in fully grasping the effects of the pandemic in the city; the central role played by public action in a situation of radical uncertainty that challenges traditional approaches to design and planning; and the need to take a stance on the urban effects of the pandemic which focuses on the dimension of everyday life and the proxemics of bodies.

This volume is a collection of reflections developed over the period spanning April 2020 to July 2021, during the most intense and tragic months of the COVID-19 pandemic.

Analyses of the geography of the virus (AGEI 2020; Bozzato 2020; Andrews et al. 2021) have shown that the pandemic more seriously affected cities and urban regions with a higher population density, although in some countries, including Italy, the initial outbreaks occurred in small- or medium-sized towns within densely populated urban regions. On the other hand, the phenomenon of the pandemic being concentrated in the most highly urbanised areas has prompted cities both to develop policies and actions capable of mitigating the most negative effects of the pandemic and to rethink their future spatial patterns and socio-economic structure in a context of radical uncertainty.

The idea of the relationship between the pandemic and socio-spatial forms of urbanisation, along with the associated challenges faced by the future of urban areas, has been the subject of a great deal of research over the past year. This complex issue has provided fertile ground for reflection not only in the field of urban planning, but also in urban studies in a broader sense, including geography, social sciences, architecture and design disciplines.

A recent and interesting survey promoted by ENI's "Enrico Mattei" Foundation (FEEM 2021; Bandarin et al. 2021), for example, suggests several lines of thinking along which to consider the complex relationship between the phenomena of global urbanisation and the current and foreseeable effects of the pandemic on the dynamics, structure and organisation of cities.

The introduction to the survey reads as follows:

> The COVID-19 crisis has had significant impacts on public health, on the lives of millions of people, and on economic development prospects at all levels, international, national, and local. All over the world, cities have been at the forefront of the crisis, as first responders to the needs of the population, as managers of the exceptional regulations needed to overcome the situation, and as promoters of the reopening and relaunching of economic and social life. The effects of the crisis will be felt for a long time, and this will require innovative responses that will see cities as protagonists (FEEM 2020: 3).

With this in mind, I will seek to offer a reflection on three families of issues. The first concerns the centrality of the socio-spatial dimension in fully grasping the effects of the pandemic in cities, with reference to the dimension of the ecological transition that is now at the heart of public action at the European scale. Space matters, especially if we wish to take a radically political view of the environmental crisis, of which the pandemic can be considered both a symptom and a consequence. Politicising the environmental crisis means linking it very intimately to the risk of seeing the socio-spatial inequalities within cities, between cities, between regions, and national states grow even further.

The second perspective has to do with our forms of rationality. The pandemic has highlighted the central role played by public action in a situation of radical uncertainty that throws an unprecedented challenge at traditional approaches to planning and programming. I would like to cast a spotlight on the need for a territorial perspective in the rethinking of development and recovery strategies, including with reference to the context offered by the implementation of the investments provided under Next Generation EU, the European project promoted at continental level in 2020 to contrast the negative effects of pandemic, and the start of the planning cycle for the EU's structural funds for the period spanning 2021–2027. My goal is to demonstrate the need for a different approach to implementing the strategies and investment programmes set to be launched in Europe over the next few years, starting with a different conceptualisation of the link between uncertainty, events and public action.

Finally, the third perspective concerns the need to take a stance on the urban effects of the pandemic which focuses on the dimension of everyday life and the proxemics of bodies. This means rethinking our cities in the wake of COVID by examining their material and symbolic effects on spatial use practices in a context characterised by a marked plurality of populations and forms of life (Pasqui 2008, 2018). Only by designing places and spaces closely connected with the relationships between individuals and groups can we truly seek to construct a different idea of the interaction between space, bodies, institutions and social relations in the post-pandemic city.

Against the backdrop of these three perspectives, this book aims to support a conscious use of knowledge, first and foremost that produced in the field of urban planning and urban studies, in a context in which the intertwining of expert knowledge and common knowledge becomes the fundamental means of producing "usable knowledge" (Lindblom and Cohen 1979). In my opinion, a critique of knowledge also represents the decisive arena for establishing the nuances of the social responsibility of expert knowledge—starting with that produced by universities—as well as effectively interpreting the social responsibility of academia in general.

The second conceptual framework that the book is built upon has been provided by the work carried out over the last three years in the context of the Departments of Excellence—"Territorial Fragilities" research project underway at the Politecnico di Milano's Department of Architecture and Urban Studies (DAStU), of which I am the scientific coordinator.

The project, which will be concluded at the end of 2022, has thus far dedicated its efforts to exploring the many and complex processes of fragilisation of the space–society relationship, with particular reference to Italy and Europe, considering territorial fragility in terms of exposure to an array of different risk and uncertainty factors: environmental, social, economic, political and institutional.

The notion of territorial fragility, which is not common in international literature, is a multidimensional concept that refers to all the various facets of a territory (land, soil, landscape)—be they geological, economic, sociopolitical, or anything in-between—and provides a metaphor that alludes to the possibility of a sudden fracture or disruption of the long-established balances and development models. It is a concept that is doubly effective: descriptive of today's complex territorial situations, characterised by great uncertainty, but also a stimulus for the development of new approaches to planning that are both integrated and multidimensional.

The sudden invasion of the pandemic into our lives has also strongly influenced the departmental project on territorial fragilities. As such, many of the reflections contained in this book can be placed in the context of the collective work carried out as part of the project. In particular, the following chapters seek, from different perspectives, to provide background on the various policies, plans and projects working to counteract the effects of the pandemic in urban areas, largely by helping to increase the preparedness and antifragility of both institutions and society when faced with undeniable conditions of radical uncertainty, which cannot be addressed solely through predictive models and risk analyses.

The post-pandemic condition of cities needs strategies, policies and projects that can contribute to a radical rethinking of models of development and forms of public action that have all very much had their limitations made clear over the past two years.

The approach used in the different chapters oscillates between theoretical reflection and operativity, including in relation to consultancy activities carried out for public administrations over this period, rooted in the awareness that only a radically experimental approach can have any hope of tackling the challenges of a radical ecological transition founded upon seeking out greater social justice for cities and territories after the pandemic.

References

AGEI (2020) Atlante COVID-19. Geografie del contagio in Italia, a cura di E. Casti, A Riggio. Roma

Andrews GJ, Crooks VA, Pearce JR, Messina JP (2021) COVID-19 and Similar Futures. Springer. Berlin

Bandarin F, Ciciotti E, Cremaschi M, Madera G, Perulli P. Shendikova D (2021) After COVID-19: a survey on the prospects for cities. City, Culture, Society, in press

Bozzato S (2020) Geografie del COVID-19. Documenti Geografici 1:5–18

FEEM (2020) Which future for cities after COVID-19. An International Survey, Fondazione "Enrico Mattei", October

Lindblom CE, Cohen DK (1979) Usable knowledge. Social science and social problem solving. Yale University Press, New Haven

Pasqui G (2008) Città, popolazioni, politiche. Jaca Book, Milano

Pasqui G (2018) La città, le pratiche, i saperi. Donzelli, Roma

Contents

Chapter 1
Uncertainty: Ontologies

Abstract This chapter reflects on the nature of radical (ontological) uncertainty produced by pandemic, that affects planning cultures, tools, strategies and practices. The difference between ontological uncertainty and risk is discussed with references to a pragmatist theory of events and relations. Moreover, the chapter proposes a theoretical approach on the options for action in post-pandemic cities, in the context of a radical possibilism.

1.1 Unpredictable Changes

What will be left on the shore once the tide of the pandemic has receded? It is difficult to say during these weeks of December 2021 in which the epidemic seems to once again be picking up steam in many parts of the world, including in Italy. On the other hand, it has been some months now since cities started coming back to life, with the urban rhythms and spaces more closely resembling those of the pre-pandemic past; however, we also seem to be living in a suspended time of sorts—a situation of deep psychological fatigue, in which uncertainty about the future shows no signs of loosening its grip.

When looking at cities, at their post-pandemic fate, we should not be too hasty in answering the question of what the short- and long-term effects will actually be (Bandarin et al. 2021). The future of urban areas, as well as of the very life forms on our planet, brings into play a crucial question regarding our inhabitation of the earth as human beings: to what extent can we predict what will happen?

For millennia, and perhaps even for a much longer period over which humans have progressively colonised the planet, the unpredictability of the future has been the defining feature of our time on the earth. In many regards, the establishment of cities partly represented—along with many other things—an attempt to reduce our levels of uncertainty, to mutually insure each other against the events that were most difficult for a more scattered human population to cope with: diseases, river floods, enemy attacks.

Since their very inception (Lanzani et al. 2020), cities have been both the space in which human beings were assigned meaning, in terms of the relationship between

G. Pasqui, *Coping with the Pandemic in Fragile Cities*, PoliMI SpringerBriefs,
https://doi.org/10.1007/978-3-030-93979-3_1

heaven and earth, and the horizontal articulation of the possibilities of common living, through planning in its earliest, embryonic forms, also understandable as the prediction and prefiguration of the possible future (be it desired or feared). The city has always acted as both a protective device and a horizon of meaning for shared living, from a cumulative perspective firmly oriented towards the future (Sini and Pasqui 2020).

From this point of view, the pandemic is most certainly not the first event to jeopardise a comprehensive and optimistic idea of the opportunities for growth and development open to both cities and their human populations. However, the crisis of the pandemic now forces us to consider cities through the lens of forms of uncertainty around the very possibility of living together, flying in the face of the sense of the urban as the coexistence of different beings within a shared, regulated space.

Thinking about this in greater depth, over the course of the last few decades, the very idea of planning—understood as the ability to forecast and plan what will happen in future with the help of increasingly sophisticated technological aids (including a nigh-unlimited mass of information and data)—has been undermined by a sequence of events and phenomena that were not entirely unpredictable, but certainly difficult to trace back to the traditional logic of risk.

The dawn of the new millennium has been heralded by three global events, all of which have taken us by surprise: the attack on the Twin Towers, the 2008 global financial crisis, and now, the pandemic. For those who knew how to listen, many signs had indicated the possibility of any of these events. With reference to the pandemic alone, David Quamenn's *Spillover* was published in 2012, and SARS (an acronym for "severe acute respiratory syndrome")—a predecessor of COVID-19—first appeared in November 2002 in the Guangdong province of China (Quamann 2012).

On the other hand, if we focus on cities and the scientific, political and design discourses that have been delivered and written about them over the last twenty years, what we leave behind is a perhaps misplaced trust in technologies as tools for reinventing urban areas with sustainability at their heart. Smart cities—to use a term that already seems somewhat passé—conveyed the idea that the most serious problems of overpopulated and polluted urban areas, the biggest casualties of the consequences of climate change, could be solved through an unprecedented alliance between the intelligence of designers, information technology and high-tech companies, with a significant (but perhaps not altogether defining) role played by institutions and citizens. The ability of both physical and virtual technologies to control and govern cities, but also to provide an improved level of urban and environmental quality for a vast number of citizens, is increasingly becoming a hot topic of critical discussion: indeed many authors refer to a "darker side of smart cities" (Balducci et al. 2019).

In this context, it is therefore perfectly legitimate to consider what permanent effects the events of the past year and a half will have on cities and territories. This question becomes all the more legitimate the more we come to terms with the fact that our ability to foresee the future, and to insure ourselves against its risks, is limited, despite humanity's extraordinary and ever-growing computational power, specifically for profound ontological reasons.

Whilst we cannot say for certain to what extent and in what specific ways this will manifest, most of us believe that in the wake of the pandemic, the forms and practices of everyday life—the organisation of labour, production and distribution processes, global interconnections and geopolitical relations—will never be able to go back to exactly the way they were, even if only due to the discourses, the cognitive and perceptual effects, and the symbolic relationships that the pandemic has produced and continues to produce.

Working on the city in a post-COVID world, or even considering how to live with this or other forms of pandemic in urban spaces, requires first and foremost a way of thinking—and perhaps an ontology—of uncertainty for at least three reasons.

The first of these is that we must learn to think about the connection between spatial relationships and the spread of viruses. Understanding the effects of the virus on different territories, and how said territories provided COVID with either fuel or resistance, has been an important research subject in the fields of urban studies and geography in recent months (AGEI 2020; Bozzato 2020). Considering Italy, for example, it has been observed that the virus initially appeared more aggressively in what some researchers have dubbed "Italia di mezzo"—"middle Italy" (Lanzani et al. 2020). The first outbreaks occurred in small towns: in Vò, in the Veneto; in Codogno, in lower Lombardy; in the Bergamo area; but also in the devastated city of Bergamo itself as well as in Cremona—and this within Lombardy alone. Medium-sized towns, periurban and diffuse urban areas, and patches of urbanized countryside: in other words, the places of the unsustainable development model that has characterised the long cycle of economic and settlement growth. We then saw the pandemic and its effects spread to major urban areas, and as we knew before and have now had confirmed, their social and spatial inequalities, as well as gaps in social and cultural capital, represent a decisive factor in whether the effects of the virus will be intensified or mitigated. Not to mention the link between interior living spaces (whether a home is large or small, the extent to which it allows for relative isolation, etc.) and collective space. The inner areas, the mountains, the depopulated villages, the places that make up this most fragile segment of Italy were the least seriously affected due to their low density, and they have now taken centre stage in a discussion around how to shape their revival in a post-urban light.

Reading the dynamics of urban areas, territories and landscapes necessarily involves seeking to truly comprehend the relationships between the virus, territorial gaps, the dynamics of development, and the forms of living at the intersection between space and society. Understanding the spatial and territorial dimension of an invisible agent may be difficult, but it is also indispensable when considering its temporary and permanent effects.

As such, the geographies of fragile territories, which are the subject of the DAStU's "Territorial Fragilities" research programme, should be used to think about how exactly the virus acts on people and families, but also on economies and practices, including with regard to an issue which should be treated with great sensitivity and resisting the pull of ideological deviations, namely the "biopolitical" effects of disciplining, confining, regulating and reducing freedom in the use of space.

The second reason why we need a new ontology of uncertainty concerns policies for the post-virus period, which will also be discussed in more depth in subsequent chapters of this book.

Even today, a year and a half after the outbreak of the pandemic, we remain unable to fully grasp and predict the effects that it will have on the Italian and world economies, but we can say with certainty that they will be dramatic, and that as a result, the urban and territorial policies at the regional, national and European scales will also be required to take this into account. The extraordinary efforts of the European Union—which we will touch upon again later—are clear evidence that the emergency sparked by COVID-19 has ushered in a new season of public action, and with it, new forms of rationality. From this point of view, it is paramount for the all the actions taken to be able to set three general objectives.

First of all, to foster the relaunch of the economy, and in particular the sectors that have been most extensively damaged by the ongoing crisis (tourism, culture, entertainment and the arts, non-food commerce, export-led sectors, manufacturing supply chains, construction, etc.) through direct support for investment also aimed at encouraging a rapid inversion of expectations and the overall economic climate, in the knowledge, however, that the pandemic is introducing certain structural changes in the forms of organisation of production and labour and that it will require us to direct our attention to certain areas in particular.

Secondly, to use structural investments as a means of creating a new model of development which revolves around the ecological conversion of the economy, as also proposed by the European Commission, which is socially and environmentally sustainable and a response to the climate transition, doing everything possible to prevent these investments for recovery from further cementing a vastly unsustainable model of development.

For example, it is crucial for any massive special maintenance operation for Italy, and for its fragile territories in particular, not to hinge upon the construction of major works, but rather to focus primarily on small infrastructure and on the maintenance and redevelopment works that will improve the quality of life of everyday citizens in a way that is immediate, both temporally and spatially. Moreover, these maintenance works could also be started and completed in a short space of time, as opposed to some large-scale projects which, as we know from experience, often have very long incubation periods. On the other hand, this model of development will inevitably need to take responsibility for establishing the digital infrastructure of the territory and providing it with the associated services (telemedicine, remote working, etc.) which equally support economic development, the reduction of inequalities and the protection of privacy.

Finally, the issue at hand is one of understanding how to use planning and implementation of the new interventions set to take place to reduce the gaps between the different parts of the country, between macro-regions, between the different fragile territories and within them. It is especially crucial to consider the growing inequalities within urban areas, making the highest priority that of supporting the groups and social classes that are most marginalised and penalised by the consequences of the pandemic. This must come with a dual focus: on the individuals and groups that are severely disadvantaged, if not in conditions of absolute poverty (this being the case for precarious workers in the low value-added tertiary sector in urban services), but also on the groups and classes that risk drastic impoverishment and a marked increase in vulnerability.

What kind of thinking and practice of public action should we deploy when designing and implementing these policies, if we assume the logic of radical uncertainty? What kind of thinking and what models of intervention do we need? This issue, which we will return to in subsequent chapters, requires an in-depth reflection on the forms of rationality of public action in conditions of radical uncertainty.

The third crucial aspect which calls for an ontology of uncertainty concerns the fundamental question posed by the pandemic: how can we live together? (Barthes 2012) As such, it is a question of understanding the deepest, most pervasive effects—those which become apparent in the everyday practices in space, forms of living, models of localised interaction, and how we exercise affectivity. It is the most uncertain and disturbing issue, but it is a thorny problem in which—once again—space matters, the most tangible and relevant forms of which are architecture and urban planning (Boeri 2021).

How are we going to tackle these shifts in imagination—shifts which the pandemic will undoubtedly induce in large sectors of the population? To what extent will they weigh on the already existing dynamics of self-immunisation and separation of populations, of spaces, even within the domestic dimension (Bassanelli 2020)? To what extent will the public regulation of space be redefined?

On this front, too, we need to propose operational hypotheses and exercises of imagination, without thinking that we can simply apply quick fixes and easy remedies; to propose policies and projects that also consider the pandemic an opportunity to rethink what it is that unites us, that "common" that defines the space of urban coexistence.

In order to truly address these challenges, to seek to respond to these questions, we must start by producing a new conceptual toolbox that attempts to take on the ineliminable and radical uncertainty that characterises the urban condition.

1.2 Risk and Uncertainty in Planning

A first move would be to think of a city not as a collection of objects (people, buildings, technologies, spaces and places), but as an arena for events. This means thinking about cities through the lens of relationships (Amin and Thrift 2002, 2016) and producing a design concept that works effectively with an urban ontology of events and relationships. An ontology of this nature must take uncertainty as its central theme.

It seems to be universally agreed that planning and design of urban policies concern the future and the possibility of changing it, and that for this reason, plans and policies have a relationship with uncertainty that is neither contingent nor incidental. Whether we define (urban) planning as a form of institutional technology for spatial control (Mazza et al. 2017) or we treat it as a variant of urban design (and in both cases, we would be referring to "physical" planning: Taylor 1998); or, indeed, we understand it as a general methodology for making rational decisions, its ultimate goal is to "reduce uncertainty". To reduce it for the operators (landowners or developers), yes, but also for citizens and society as a whole; or perhaps to reduce it for the decision-maker, through an attempt to achieve a given final state by coordinating a collection of activities.

Even in its most common sense, planning implies the ability to foresee and orient reality in order to outline possible future states of the world, and precisely for this reason, it is a complex activity, because past, present and future are not fully known to anyone and are all characterised—albeit in different ways by uncertainty (Moroni and Cozzolino 2020).

In economic theory, uncertainty refers to situations in which contingency and randomness cannot be expressed in terms of probability, whilst risk concerns settings in which the person who takes a decision can assign a subjective probability to different courses of events (Knight 1933). From this perspective, risk can be internalised in probabilistic forecasting models, whereas ontological uncertainty is the other side of the unpredictability of the world and the insuperable limits of human knowledge.

Rational choice theory has developed the distinction between the two in considerable depth, highlighting how situations of uncertainty play a central role when interaction between different individuals comes into play (Kreps 1988).

Every planner is well aware that her/his problem is not risk at least in this economic/statistical sense—but rather uncertainty. We do not know a great deal about the future, nor do we know much about the present or the past. When we attempt to design systems of rules, institutions, even physical objects, not only are we faced with situations about which we do not have detailed and certain knowledge, but also—and above all—we are forced to deal with different actors (driven by interests that are often conflicting or at the very least contradictory) who produce a vast amount of knowledge to be considered. As Charles E. Lindblom wrote:

> ordinary citizens, politicians and other public officials, heads of private organizations, opinion leaders, and experts of various kinds, including, for special attention, scientists […] set or define problems, think about and establish goals, find opportunities, cope with complexity, seek or take advantage of information, inform and misinform each other, and create answers when they cannot discover them (Lindblom 1990: vii).

As such, planning processes are not merely complex because the rationality of the actors is limited, but more so because they involve "fields of interrelated practices"—dynamics of social interaction that introduce different interests, forms of rationality and values into the mix.

What's more, in planning practices which bring into play significant and conflicting issues, we can observe fully-fledged "dissent" (a condition of *differend*, to quote Lyotard 1988), in which discursive regimes and incommensurable forms of rationality end up not even finding common ground between them.

Uncertainty involved in urban planning processes often has this "wicked" nature (Rittel and Webber 1973)—a nature from which no technical or scientific knowledge, however neutral it is imagined to be, can liberate us. And it is on this stage that the substance of the events themselves takes place.

In an article from a few years ago devoted specifically to the issue of uncertainty in planning, John Abbott wrote that uncertainty is created by the changing social environment or planning context (Abbott 2005). This means that we can distinguish between two forms of uncertainty: process-related uncertainty and context-related uncertainty. Whilst according to Abbott, the former depends on uncertainty regarding the external environment, the value judgements at play and the future intentions of the actors, the latter is characterised by four dimensions, which Abbott calls casual, human and organizational, external (related to wider social environment) and chance uncertainty" (Abbott 2005: 242). This last dimension, he explains, refers to "truly unknowable one-off chance events" (*ibid.*).

As such, events form an essential component of any uncertainty that "comes from outside", in that it has to do with contextual dimensions that are uncontrollable and unforeseeable. The consequence that Abbott draws from these considerations is both surprising and interesting:

> Effective planning is a risky and uncertain process, [and] to change the future and reduce environmental uncertainty, organizations and individuals involved in the process, including professional planners, need to push the bounds of possibility – paradoxically, this will raise process uncertainty and the risk of disagreement and failure (Abbott 2005: 249–250).

The situation that the pandemic has put us in is located precisely within the theoretical place recognised by Abbott: planning has to do with events, but it cannot ever hope to internalise them completely in its predictions.

1.3 Practices and Events

So how can we deal with events, such as this pandemic, under conditions of radical uncertainty? First of all, we should take stock of the fact that:

> the word 'uncertain' means that there is something, be it a judgement or an event, in which we cannot 'distinguish' what is true from what is false, or also what will (truly) occur from what will not (truly) occur. Uncertainty, in this sense, refers to a lack of knowledge and, more specifically, to situations in which we know the type of consequences but cannot meaningfully attribute probabilities to the occurrence of the event entailing such consequences (Chiffi and Chiodo 2020: 6).

Moreover, in order to contend with this uncertainty—which has the nature of the event—we must look at it from a dual perspective.

On the one hand, by imagining that in pluralistic and fragmented societies, uncertainty (and with it the events that it entails) is associated with the activation of probing processes, assuming public action as a practice of social inquiry (Dewey 1927; 1929; Lindblom 1990).

On the other hand, by accepting the uncertainty of events in all its radicality, thus acknowledging that planning is not a technical or managerial activity. It is a "field", in the sense coined by Pierre Bourdieu (2013), in which different kinds of practices are intertwined and in which systems of power and knowledge interact and compete with one another (Foucault 1980).

The practical turn in social sciences, philosophy and epistemology (Galison 1987; Latour 1987) starts from the assumption of the plural nature of practices. In this perspective, practice is not a distinct field of experiences defined oppositely with respect to theory. Theories, knowledges, concepts are produces inside practices, and disciplines, with their own specific objects and methodologies, should be described as complex interactions between different practices.

Practices are actions in which our doing happens in a continuous process of transformation that establishes meaning and produces multiple effects. In this sense, practices are not variants of Aristotelian *praxis*, as a faculty or activity opposite to theory (Anscombe 1965). According to a line of reflection that has its roots in American pragmatism (Knorr-Cetina 1996) and which today also appears influential in the reflection on planning (Healey 2009), theory itself is a field of practices, of different nature, in which knowledge is inextricably intertwined.

According to Italian philosopher Carlo Sini (2009)

> the habit of practice, that having to do that in every moment characterizes being a living and working subject (...) attends certain thresholds; these determinations are summarized and ideally included in the word 'practice'. It is about life practices and knowledge, or, in general terms, it is about knowing how to do, knowing how to say, knowing how to write. 'Practice' is thus what the subject is immersed in from time to time (Sini 2004: 27).

The subjects are "immersed" in the practices because they are able to concretely inhabit the situations and contexts in which they find themselves. When we act, we are often not acting as rational subjects; we act unintentionally, being dependent from the practices we are immersed in. For instance, our routines, what we do (and how we do it) in relation to a background of meaning for which we know how to do it (as everyone does). In this sense, practices are linked with processes of sensemaking. References to organizational theorists (Weick 1995; Wenger 1998) who have worked on practices as "sensible" routines (of doing and how we get over it) are therefore pertinent to an idea of practice such as "what people he does and brings to completion with the intention of doing it: without making a problem of it each time, because he has already done it this way and this is how it is done, since everyone does it that way" (Sini 2004: 28).

Practices never happen in isolation from each other; they cooperate in a "synesthesia" that only an analytical gaze can unravel. "A practice is therefore an intertwining of many practices, subordinated to the pre-eminent purpose of the practice, that is, to the achievement of its objects. (...). The final purpose (coinciding with the establishment of its threshold in action) or what is targeted in the establishment of the threshold of practice, is the 'transcendental' element of the practice: what structures its overall meaning and orders its end, articulating the intermediate elements" (Sini 2004: 30).

Summing up, Sini's description of the practices has three main ingredients. First, there is no pure practice: each practice is an (infinite) intertwining of a multiplicity of practices, some of which are primary, others secondary to the object (for the "transcendental" purpose) of the practice.

Second, every practice is social, even when it is apparently isolated, even as it is inherited and learned through imitation and example. The practice happens in this horizon together with its meaning, redefining, even imperceptibly, the framework of meaning.

Third, each practice has a purpose. The purpose of the practice is its object, the reason why we start acting, often unintentionally. For this reason,the thought of practices is a thought of effects and not of intentions, of outcomes and not of choices. However, finalization occurs at the intersection between subjectivation and the constitution of objects.

1.4   Events and Relations

So how can we deal with events, such as this pandemic, under conditions of radical uncertainty? From the point of view of practices, then, uncertainty is intimately bound to events because, in the "transit" of one practice into another, each practice generates *new meanings* which can, in turn, be thought of as events (of the practice itself).

But what does event mean, in a definitive sense? We already know that in the public discourse on the city and its transformations, we can interpret the term in two ways. On the one hand, events are understood as "occasions", as opportunities for development and the attraction of people and investments. There are countless examples of this: from the Olympic Games to world expositions, with any number of film, theatre or literary festivals in-between. These events, however, cannot actually be designated as uncertain.

On the other hand, events are defined as any natural or social happenings that are (more or less) unpredictable and/or catastrophic. In this case, events are associated with situations of risk (be it "terrorism risk", "seismic risk" or, as we now see, "pandemic risk") out of which some dramatic situation may arise, its effects largely indeterminate. The examples that immediately spring to mind ultimately allow us to say that these are events to which we can potentially attempt to engage in resignification or sensemaking activities, under certain conditions.

Ultimately, both current uses of "event" can present some interesting connections with planning processes. However, perhaps we need a more precise definition of the term "event" if we are to reflect upon its possible use in such processes.

The concept of an event is one of the most complex in philosophy and the social sciences. I shall therefore settle for providing a mere outline of two possible theoretical meanings of event, taking my cues from an article published in a British journal by French philosopher Alain Badiou (2007) dedicated to the difference between his conception of an event and that offered by Gilles Deleuze (1995; 2015).

According to Badiou, Deleuze proposes a theory that considers the event to be something quite ordinary. For Deleuze, events are "the ontological realization of the eternal truth of the One, the infinite power [*puissance*] of Life". The event "would not be what takes place between a past and a future, between the end of a world and the beginning of another" (Badieu 2007: 38). Deleuze's events are continuous— they are the occurrence of practices in their "transit" and their "threshold", along the "plane of immanence" that characterises them. For Badiou, quite the opposite is true: the event is the uncertain, risky and rare transition from one state of the worls to another. It is "a pure break with the becoming of an object of the world, through the auto-apparition of this object. [...] The event extracts from a time the possibility of an other time" (Badiou, 2007: 39). Deleuze considers events to be the continuous occurrence of the immanence of life as it happens; Badiou sees them as a break that generates new possibilities of and for the world.

If we want to reflect on the possible use of events in planning practices, both understandings of what an event is can prove useful to us. In one case (Deleuze's event), planning intercepts events as one practice slips into another, in the contin- uous process of resignification, the network of which constitutes its process. From this perspective, each practice is a complex network of infinite practices, and each occurrence of transference from one practice to another takes the form of an event on the plane of immanence (where all practices are "horizontal"). Consequently, plan- ning is uncertain not (only) because our knowledge is so limited, but (also) because we live within the flow of practices, more or less unconsciously attending its events and openings, which are first and foremost processes of resignification (of objects and subjects).

On the other hand, Badiou's theory also provides us with a rather useful conception of the event. In this second line of thinking, the planning process can incorporate a radical redefinition, a break in the continuum which gives rise to entirely new meanings. The event is a new beginning, surprising and unpredictable, which forces all actors involved to relocate and invent themselves within the process. In the latter case, the event is a "catastrophe", in the sense offered by René Thom (1989). It demands a radical redefinition of the planning process, lest the action end up being wholly ineffective.

Events, in both senses, are very familiar to planners. Immanent events, in Deleuze's sense, occur in practices on a daily basis; in fact, more accurately, they are the very event of practices in their occurrence and transit. Discontinuous events, in Badiou's sense, challenge the continuity and linearity of processes by forcing all actors involved to undertake their own reframing (Schön and Rein 1994).

What is important is that, in both cases (or perhaps these are simply two ways of interpreting the same phenomenon), events are truly seen as "occasions" in that they are opportunities to learn and to innovate. As such, it is a question of constructing planning policies and processes which, precisely because of their exploratory nature, are porous to the event. Porous in this case means welcoming, open to the forces, to the unpredictability that is the result of the invasion of the new, but also of the continuity of the web (of meanings) of practices.

On the other hand, exposure to the event—to its radical uncertainty—is also an occasion or opportunity to build the public world. Ulrich Beck also affirmed this, in his own way, in a conference held at the London School of Economics entitled

"Living in the World Risk Society" (Beck 2006). Beck refers to the "irrepressible ubiquity of radical uncertainty in the modern world" (Beck 2006: 10). This ubiquity is evidenced by the relationship between global risks and the establishment of a global public sphere. Beck writes:

> In his 1927 book *The Public and its Problems*, John Dewey explained that not actions but consequences lie at the heart of politics. Although Dewey was certainly not thinking of global warming, BSE or terrorist attacks, his idea is perfectly applicable to world risk society. A global public discourse does not grow out of a consensus of decision, but of a dissent over the consequences of decisions. Modern risk crises are constituted by just such controversies over consequences. Where some may see an overreaction to risk, it is also possible to see grounds for hope. Because such risk conflicts do indeed have an enlightenment function (Beck 2006: 339).

Events, and with them the ability to construct policies and processes that are porous and permeable to them, therefore also represent an opportunity to generate public involvement in planning processes, understood as social inquiry practices. This means creating the conditions for openness to social innovation, but also seriously accepting the fact that events are unpredictable and radically "other"—that they are opportunities in the Greek sense of *kairos*.

What kind of ontology underpins this conception of the event under conditions of radical uncertainty? In my opinion, an ontology of relationships, along a line of thinking that connects American pragmatism, specifically transactionalism (Dewey 1929) with Norman Whitehead's reflections on reality as a process (Whitehead 1979) and certain authors of contemporary Italian and French philosophy (Deleuze 1995; Sini 2009).

An ontology of relationships is, in the first instance, a way of thinking that conceives of the relationship before its objective poles, and that therefore identifies the relationship as the hinge of a worldview centred on connections rather than entities (including the individual).

The pandemic has given us a tangible demonstration of how urban space is first and foremost a space of relationships. Relationships between humans, above all, but also between humans and other living beings (animals and plants), and with objects, technologies, information flows. Each relationship occurs in the context of practices, which are in turn complex assemblages of things and words, objects and discourses. The literature has now firmly established an interpretation of the urban as a socio-technical system (Amin and Thrift 2016). As I see it, these systems are practices interwoven with one another, pieced together from heterogeneous traits both material and immaterial in nature and never existing in isolation.

Why does an ontology of relationships appear to be more consistent with a conception based on radical uncertainty? Because it imagines the event as the occurrence of new relationships, as seen from a specific perspective (by an "interpretant", to use the language of Charles Sanders Peirce). Uncertainty defines the occurrence of the event itself—its coming into being on the basis of a context of meaning and a field of practices that is continuously redefining its possible relationships. In this sense, the crucial point is to understand the potential relationships, the new assemblages based on which "things" (including human individuals) happen in relationships.

A reflection on the options for action in the context of a radical possibilism is the task that the pandemic event presents us with.

References

Abbott J (2005) Understanding and managing the unknown. The nature of uncertainty in planning. J Plan Educ Res 24:237–251

AGEI (2020) Atlante Covid-19. Geografie del contagio in Italia, a cura di E. Casti, A Riggio. Roma

Amin A, Thrift N (2002) Cities, reimagining the urban. Polity Press, London

Amin A, Thrift N (2016) Seeing like a city. Polity Press, London

Anscombe GEM (1965) Thought and action in Aristotle. In: Bambrough R (ed) New essays on Plato and Aristotle. Routledge, London and New York, pp 143–158

Balducci A, Karimi M, Kunzmann K (2019) The darker side of smart city development. Urbanistica 163:91–95

Badiou A (2007) The event in Deleuze. Parrhesia 2:37–44

Bandarin F, Ciciotti E, Cremaschi M, Madera G, Perulli P, Shendikova D (2021) After Covid-19: a survey on the prospects for cities. City, Culture, Society, in press

Barthes R (2012) How to live together. Columbia University Press, New York

Bassanelli M (ed) (2020) Covid Home. Luoghi e modi dell'abitare, dalla pandemia in poi, Lettera 22, Siracusa

Beck U (2006) Living in the world risk society. Econ Soc 35(3):329–345

Boeri S (2021) Urbania. Laterza, Bari

Bourdieu P (2013) Outline of a theory of practice. Cambridge University Press, Cambridge (UK)

Bozzato S (2020) Geografie del Covid-19. Documenti Geografici 1:5–18

Chiffi D, Chiodo S (2020), Risk and uncertainty. Foundational issues. In Balducci A, Chiffi D, Curci F (eds) Risk and resilience. Springer Brief, Berlin-Milano, pp 1–13

Deleuze G (1995) Difference and repetition. Columbia Univ. Press, New York

Deleuze G (2015) Logic of sense. Bloomsbury Academics, New York

Dewey J (1927) The public and its problems. Holt, New York

Dewey J (1929) The quest for certainty: a study of the relation of knowledge and action. Minton Balch & Co., New York

Foucault M (1980) Power/knowledge: selected interviews and other writings, 1972–1977. Pantheon Books, New York

Galison P (1987) How experiments end. University of Chicago Press, Chicago

Healey P (2009) The pragmatic tradition in planning theory. J Plan Educ Res 28(3):277–292

Knight FH (1933) Risk, uncertainty and profit. Oxford University Press, Oxford

Knorr-Cetina KD (1996) The manufacture of knowledge. Pergamon, Oxford

Kreps D (1988) Notes on the theory of choice. Westview Press, Boulder

Lanzani A, De Leo D, Mattioli C, Morello E, Zanfi E (2020) Nell'Italia di mezzo: rigenerazione e valorizzazione dei territori della produzione. In: Coppola A, Del Fabbro M, Lanzani A, Pessina G, Zanfi F (a cura di) Ricomporre i divari. Politiche e progetti territoriali contro le disuguaglianze e per la transizione ecologica. Il Mulino, Bologna, pp 107–116

Latour B (1987) Science in action. Open University Press, Milton Keynes

Lindblom C (1990) Inquiry and change. Yale University Press, New Haven

Lyotard J-F (1988) The differend. University of Minnesota Press, Minneapolis

Mazza L, Gaeta L, Janin U (2017) Governo del territorio e pianificazione spaziale. Città studi, Milano

Moroni S, Cozzolino S (2020) Conditions of actions in complex socio-spatial systems. In: de Roo G, Yamu C, Zuidema C (eds) Handbook on planning and complexity. Edward Elgar Publishing, Northampton, pp 186–202

Quamann D (2012) Spillover. W W Norton & Co Inc., New York

Rittel HW, Webber M (1973) Dilemmas in a general theory of planning. Policy Sci 4(2):155–169

Schön D, Rein M (1994) Frame reflection. Basic Books, New York

Sini C (2004) L'analogia della parola. Jaca Book, Milano.

Sini C (2009) Ethics of writings. SUNY Press, Albany (NY)

Sini C, Pasqui G (2020) Perché gli alberi non rispondono. Lo spazio urbano e i destini dell'abitare. Jaca Book, Milano

Thom R (1989) Structural stability and morphogenesis: an outline of a general theory of models. Addison-Wesley, Reading (MA)

Weick KE (1995) Sensemaking in organisations. Sage Publications, Thousand Oaks (CA)

Wenger E (1998) Communities of practice, learning, meaning and identity. Cambridge University Press, Cambridge (Mass)

Whitehead NA (1979) Process and reality. Free Press, New York

Chapter 2
Ecology: Politics

Abstract The chapter moves from the hypothesis that the environmental issues connected with pandemic should be considered at the same time political issues. Through a discussion of the international literature on political ecology, the chapter introduces an analysis of the connections between the ecological dimension of COVID-19 pandemic and the growing socio-spatial inequalities in urban areas. The chapter discusses and criticize the "anti-urban" perspective emerging in discussion about post-pandemic, and proposes to reimagine a new development model for cities and territories that combines socio-spatial justice and ecological transition.

2.1 Political Ecology

The urban issue as an environmental issue is either political or it is not. This may seem like a bold and excessively radical statement, but I believe that it is an observation rooted in what has happened in the period between our situation today and the terrible spread of the pandemic in Italy and around the world, the daily deaths, the catastrophe of the government of public health (above all in Lombardy, my region), the haphazard management of the vaccination campaign.

The underlying reason for this necessary intertwining of the environmental dimension and socio-political issues is quite simple to identify: in short, the pandemic was a catalyst, accelerating processes that were already underway, both on a global scale and within Italy. Processes in which the spread of the virus and the manifestation of its effects in cities concretely demonstrated the connection between global transformations and socio-technological assemblages.

The work of international literature known as "Political Ecology" now seems relevant at a time when the rhetoric of the ecological transition and sustainability occasionally tends to obscure the markedly political and conflictual nature of the environmental crisis in the way it has also emerged in relation to the pandemic. As Benjaminsen and Svarstad write:

> is a field within environmental studies focusing on power relations as well as the coproduction of nature and society. Theoretical inspirations are taken from different sources such as political economy, poststructuralism, and peasant studies. Contributions to this field tend to

question the status of powerful actors (e.g., governments, businesses, conservation organiza-
tions) and what is taken for granted in leading discourses (Benjaminsen and Svarstad 2019:
391).

Political ecology has also found extensive application in the specific field of urban
studies:

Urban political ecology combines elements of urban ecology and political ecology. It seeks
to expose the complex socioecological relationships that shape urban environments. It can
be understood as a political-economy of urban systems, but focusing on the environmental
aspects of the city. In this sense, it builds on a long tradition of academic research into
human–Nature relationships that have led to the construction of urban environments. Within
urban political economy there is a focus on power and how it is exercised in shaping the
city and the lives of people, and other species, in the city. This involves both structures and
individual actions. The political ecology background is predominantly Marxist, or at least
Marxist-inspired, and builds on earlier Marxist urban geography. There are many different
and sometimes overlapping approaches within urban political ecology, including those that
emphasize urban metabolisms, those that challenge neoliberalism as a system of governance,
and those that focus on a particular issue, such as water, poverty, or transport (McManus
2009: 295).

On the other hand, the radical nature of the environmental crisis has its roots in the
anthropological transformation that has been underway for at least two centuries—
which Friedrich Nietzsche, for example, had lucidly prophesied when he referred
to the definitive fracturing of the "man-nature unit" (Nietzsche 2019)—following
a path which has maintained the traits of globalisation and technology production
taken from the Greek origins of Western civilisation.

In an attempt to trace a few elements of these long-term dynamics, I will draw
upon a short book by Michel Serres, a prolific and visionary thinker who recently
passed away. The book (Serres 2009), written as a reflection on the financial crisis
sparked after 2007, starts by recognising six events which had been a long time in the
making but which emerged with explosive force in the second half of the twentieth
century. These are events that concern the slow and heavy rhythm of the relationship
between man, earth and technology: the rhythm that has marked every step along the
way of the configuration of the human being and the birth of culture since its earliest
origins (Sini, Pievani 2020).

The first event is the largest ever instance of population movement in history,
which is first and foremost a migration from the countryside to the cities. Serres
describes it thus: "Although it continues to feed itself thanks to the earth, Western
humanity has abandoned it" (Serres 2009: p.14). There are two consequences to this
abandonment: on the one hand, the entire world itself becomes urbanized, and in
this sense, given the historical connection between cities and political dimensions
of human being, "everything is political". On the other, and consequently, the world
is taking its revenge and threatening humanity. The ecological catastrophe is not
the result of a spontaneous process, but rather depends directly upon the processes
of anthropisation and urbanisation. Serres states that the consequence of becoming
aware of this fact is recognising that nothing will ever truly be political again, at least
not in the traditional sense. The eminently political dimension of ecology (Bryant
2015; Perreault et al. 2015) has its roots here.

The second event is total mobilisation made possible by technological innovations in the transportation sector. Never before have goods, people or information moved along the surface of the planet—and even through its atmosphere—with this intensity and speed. It is no coincidence that the ability to move around is increasingly becoming the condition of citizenship everywhere, on a local and a global scale (Urry 2007; Mezzadra and Neilson 2013). In unsettlingly prophetic words, Serres wrote: "This movement exposes the human immune system to pandemics that we may one day no longer know how to address" (Serres 2009; 18).

The third event has to do with the at once extraordinary and disturbing development of life science and healthcare technologies, the intensive use of which produces human (but also animal and vegetable) bodies that differ considerably from those of our ancestors, even our recent ones. Mutating bodies, in which the meaning of inhabiting the rhythms of the cosmos and the earth is fading away.

The fourth event, which is closely linked to the previous one, and more specifically to the differentiated yet generalised increase in life expectancy and the reduction in infant mortality, ultimately gives us the most dramatic demographic shift in history. Exponential population growth in some parts of the planet, sudden ageing in others: nothing short of another world, a world which the devastating COVID-19 mortality statistics has opened our eyes to in the most tragic and immediate of ways.

The fifth event concerns the way in which we live together—our relationships and connections. Serres speaks of the "collective" (which had essentially sustained us throughout the "short century", with all its dreams and nightmares) being replaced with the "connective", which on the one hand allows us to establish and maintain relationships over long distances (the Internet and social media spring to mind, of course, but big data and its pervasive use is also relevant), and on the other radically transforms the forms and means of producing and reproducing knowledge, horizontalising it and putting an end to the social reputation of expertise. Needless to say, these phenomena have become visible over these long months of mindless chatter between countless "experts".

We come, finally, to the sixth event, namely the development of military and nuclear technologies making humans more dangerous than ever before to their fellow human beings. The fate of the planet and our species—and even its end—are for the first time in our hands and in our power to command.

Six interrelated events at the intersection of technological change (information science and life sciences), demographic shift and social transition. It is against this backdrop that the drama of the pandemic unfolded; against this backdrop that we fully appreciate the sense of radical uncertainty in which we are called upon to plan and organise.

Whilst the spread of COVID-19 has shed a bright light on the glaring failings of a model of global capitalism that is incapable of insuring and reinsuring itself against risk (not only as regards pandemics, but also in relation to the unpredictable effects of climate change), the events of the past year and a half have once again shifted the focus squarely onto the issue of the public sector, of the role and significance of public action in the regulation, governance and design of our societies, and in particular the city, the territory and the landscape. What is happening to us, in government and urban practices, is a predominantly cultural crisis stemming from the idea that all problems in society can be solved by the market or by society itself, without—or even against—the public sector.

If we consider Italy in particular, the somewhat justified ill repute of public policies and action offers us a concrete system of action in which all the actors (politicians, technostructures, bureaucracies) put all their fragility on show. Abandoning the idea that public intervention is a problem is not a matter for cultural debate. The stakes are unspeakably high: the balances of power on a worldwide scale, practices of control and domination that have intensified deep inequalities (Piketty 2015), power relations between social classes and crises of agency for any and all radically alternative perspectives, both in nation states and at the global level. However, breaking free of the lexicon and the atmosphere that have dominated public discourse at this crucial moment, as capitalist globalisation is poised to reach its peak, is merely one of the necessary conditions. We will return to these issues in more detail in Chaps. 6 and 7 of this book.

2.2   The Answer is in the Cities

Having accepted that the pandemic has amplified various interconnected aspects (the environmental crisis as a political issue, the deep-rooted nature of territorial dispari-ties and social inequalities, the reconstruction of the centrality of public action), it is then a question of understanding what the crucial issues are in our attempts to find not a way of leaving cities, but a different way of living in them.

To achieve this, as already hinted at in the previous chapter, we must first think of cities as complex artefacts and, at the same time, as fields of interrelated practices. Taking our cues from Amin and Thrift (2016), it is therefore a matter of looking at the pandemic and its issues "through the eyes of the city". This means considering the world's cities in their tangible and intangible interactions, as interrelated fields of technologies, objects (both natural and social), practices and social relationships. The concept of the socio-technical system, wherein technologies and objects are attached to specific practices, connected in networks of meanings, assimilated into apparatuses of knowledge and power, allows us to understand that the urban effects of the pandemic exist within a highly dynamic context, one in which the role and characteristics of the urban are being redesigned (Brenner 2004). Only by observing the relationship between the city and the pandemic in this way can we truly grasp the nature and meaning of being a city in the post-pandemic scenario, without invoking palingenetic changes and, at the same time, without underestimating the possible permanent effects of the dynamics at work.

A 2008 text written by sociologists S. Harris Ali and Roger Keil in the wake of the SARS outbreak traces the relationships between the flows of money, raw mate-rials and people that led to the spread of this infectious disease between Hong Kong, Singapore and Toronto. In doing so, the authors ultimately demonstrate that the

vulnerability of these three global cities was a direct consequence of the global interconnections and models of urban development (Quamann 2012) that had produced
woefully inadequate forms of governance and healthcare infrastructure, long before
the virus ever spread (Harris Ali and Keil 2008).

As Paola Piscitelli writes:

> we are seeing the tragic reality first-hand, namely that access to healthcare is not equal for
> everyone, and that health and environmental crises have a discriminatorily disproportionate
> effect on populations, inextricably linked as they are with the interpretation of power relations
> and class, gender or ethnic struggles. Health crises such as the one currently taking place and
> the environmental crises from which they stem are fundamentally political issues (Piscitelli
> 2020: 1).

From this point of view, the resilience of cities and attempts to counteract the
dramatic effects of the pandemic cannot be associated with "anti-urban" perspectives.
Of course, certain phenomena involving the relocation of work may redefine the
attractiveness of areas far outside cities (inner areas, touristic residential areas), but
on the whole, the dynamics of urban concentration—especially for service sectors
and for lower-income social groups—are not reversible in the short term.

For this reason, we cannot espouse any sort of apocalyptical rhetoric that would
hold the pandemic up as an event destined to radically overhaul our ways of life and
our forms of using space, the organisation of production, distribution and consumption, our mobility practices and settlement structures. This perspective imagines that
cities will never be the same again; that ultimately, the pandemic will deliver us to
a future of less dense, more rarefied settlements, as well as a new proxemics of our
relationships in public.

Some have even gone so far as to imagine, and propose, a deliberate counter
urbanisation: an exodus from the cities to the inner and marginal areas, a reclama-
tion of our abandoned villages. These villages, however, bear an unsettling resem-
blance to gentrified neighbourhoods, occupied by a creative class that is perma-
nently connected through their technological devices. The development of inner and
marginal areas, including as regards post-pandemic dynamics, requires an altogether
different conception of the possible balances to be struck between the places to be
reinhabited and the economic and social forms of urban development (De Rossi
2018).

Others are envisaging cities in which we will experience a completely different
way of life, technologically, aesthetically and socially. Indeed, much of the prevailing
rhetoric on smart cities considers this fertile ground on which to pave the way for
new markets and new forms of consumption. Even the edifying and pervasive matter
of the Sustainable Development Goals, as promoted by the United Nations in 2015,
can serve to obfuscate the role of the powerful interests hiding behind the rhetoric
of technological innovation at the urban scale.

I am by no means convinced that the two years since the start of the pandemic
has provided any solid arguments for this "anti-urban" narrative; instead, at the first
opportunity, the same old conditioned reflexes have been set in motion, and the same
old deeply entrenched behaviours have resurfaced. We have used our cars more

intensively in the city, to name but one example. We have given up on the much-heralded comprehensive and detailed reflection on the reorganisation of local public transportation. We have prioritised the issues of trade and the economy over those of education, closing schools whilst opening shopping centres as soon as possible.

On the other hand, there is also a different emotional tone at play which imagines quite the opposite, namely that the crisis will pass without leaving too many traces, much as other epidemics throughout history have done. This second perspective assumes that the settlement patterns and the structure of our societies and territories will not change in any significant way and that ultimately, everything will (more or less) go back to the way it was before.

We all know that the world's economies and urban markets will all take a hit from a severe crisis, although it is not easy at the moment to offer any reasonable forecasts about the macroeconomic dynamics of the coming months and years: it is precisely for this reason that restarting our engines as soon as possible is so crucial. Much of the rhetoric that was mobilised—often inappropriately—during the initial phase of the crisis points in this direction, along with various social and economic forces. Business as usual, then.

2.3   Inequalities and Ecological Transition

The repoliticisation of the environmental crisis and the dismantling of the rhetoric of sustainability represent two moves used to connect environmental and social issues against the backdrop of the pandemic. The subject was raised emphatically by Bruno Latour in his proposal to overhaul politics on a planetary scale, starting from the notion of the "terrestrial" (Latour 2017).

Now more than ever—argues Latour—it is abundantly clear that the issue of politics and the issue of science are two sides of the same problem: it is only through a profound rethinking of the idea of nature, i.e. by rejecting its presumed otherness, our conception of it as mute and objective, and instead accepting its ethical and political significance, that we can arrive at a new model for societies and ecosystems. In other words, social policies and environmental policies are different responses to the same problem.

This perspective constitutes a clear break with both the long-established traditions of the left-wing political and trade union forces over the course of the twentieth century—which struggle to abandon a paradigm centred around development understood as growth—and the depoliticising, and ultimately neutralising, conceptions of sustainability.

In a recent book edited by Alessandro Coppola, Matteo Del Fabbro, Arturo Lanzani, Gloria Pessina and Federico Zanfi (*Ricomporre i divari*: *Bridging the Gaps*; Coppola et al. 2021), the result of a collective research project incubated in the DAStU's "Territorial Fragilities" programme at the Politecnico di Milano, the closely intertwined issues of the fight against inequalities and the ecological transition have been placed at the heart of more than twenty proposals for Italian cities and territories that are both visionary and functional.

It is an important book, in that it shows that the stakes in the construction of a new perspective of development for Italy and Europe include a massive redistribution of power, which would affect vested interests.

The development of the volume was founded upon a general and powerful observation: the inequalities between individuals and social groups, which have grown enormously over recent decades on a global scale (Picketty 2015), are at once social and spatial phenomena, and as such can only be adequately interpreted if we understand the territorial gaps within which these inequalities, along with the resulting social injustice (Soja 2010; Fainstein 2011; Secchi 2013).

This is precisely why the issue of inequalities plays such an important role when it comes to interpreting territorial fragilities, particularly in the wake of the pandemic. Fragility also has a demographic, social and economic component to be considered. The fragility of territories, landscapes, ecologies, human settlements and nature, both within and outside our most intensively urbanised environments, are intimately linked to human activity, to the models of development that we have adopted, the unsustainability of which is becoming increasingly apparent.

This form of unsustainability has to do with the breakdown of the age-old relationship between the human species and nature, which I previously mentioned with reference to the work of Michel Serres (2001), and which has been concretely represented by the demographic and technological acceleration of the last hundred years, with close links to processes of reorganisation and rearrangement of economic and political powers on a global scale. With this in mind, considering territorial inequalities and attempting to bridge the gaps means calling into question a development model on a national and international scale, suspending our faith in the self-regulatory abilities of an economic and social formation—namely that of financially-driven globalised capitalism—that has increasingly resulted in the standardisation of places and spaces.

This form of society, with all its powers, discourses and institutions, now including during the devastating pandemic, but even before it, when faced with the global environmental crisis—no longer proves to be capable of insuring and reinsuring itself against unpredictable events. As we have increasingly come to understand over these last few months and as we saw in the previous chapter, these are events characterised by radical uncertainty which also require new forms of rationality and a strong ability to experiment. This is the inescapable background against which we must also place the efforts of public policies and projects: efforts in which the environmental crisis and territorial policies are intimately bound.

Rooted in a long-standing tradition of interpreting the Italian territory, the development of the "Ricomporre i divari" ("Bridging the Gaps") project reminds us that we have to take an incisive and multi-scalar look at the variations between territories, at the way in which the relationships between the different dimensions of fragility, the different gaps and inequalities, manifest themselves across Italy's various territories.

It is precisely for these reasons—for the attention devoted to establishing a top-down view, but also up-close, direct observation, for the ability to combine an academic knowledge of places with a certain care-passion, even—for people and populations—that the "Ricomporre i divari" project has proven capable of producing usable knowledge.

Usable does not necessarily mean mechanically applicable, however. The proposals gathered around the four axes—territorial strategies, housing policies, infrastructure for everyday life, and mobility networks and services have different degrees of immediate practicability. As Pier Luigi Crosta often reminds us, research being usable does not necessarily mean that it is applicable in an immediate and utilitarian way (Crosta and Bianchetti 2021).

That said, the proposals set out in Coppola et al. (2021) are very concrete and implementable, and it seems as though they share three essential features. First of all, policies aimed at combating inequalities must prioritise a representation and a theory for dealing with the problem of territorial disparities. Policies are not effective if they are not territorial, as blatantly demonstrated not only by the phase of management of the health crisis into which we have been plunged, but also the current attempts at strategic orientation in the use of EU resources. In order to construct truly territorial policies, we must first overturn a dominant culture found amongst social and political forces and in our institutions, as well as offering policymakers and stakeholders the tools to comprehend that varying actions by territory can ensure the right combination of effectiveness, efficiency and appropriateness. Truly place-based policies adapted specifically to suit given territories can also be managed more effectively because they are more participatory, more sensitive to the dimension of the real-world effects on the material lives of people and communities.

In order to achieve this—as explicitly mentioned by many of the projects—we also need a different form of public administration, a sense of authority for the public sector, which so desperately needs financial resources, but also cognitive resources and intelligent working methods. After decades of disrepute for the public sector, the current situation clearly shows the need to bolster public action at both the national and local levels. The financial, organizational and cognitive weakening of public actors has greatly reduced the effectiveness—as well as the efficiency of public action, which has also been dogged by the growing bureaucratisation of administrative action, which is in turn justified by the necessary struggle against corruption.

In this context, we also need adequate technical knowledge. Rethinking our educational pathways, freeing their design and experimentation from the bureaucratic oppression that stands in the way of allowing the energy and resources found predominantly in universities to truly blossom, is a significant step towards re-establishing the link between education, policies and visions for the future.

The second aspect that I would like to highlight is that the proposals contained in "Ricomporre i divari" are oriented towards outlining specific policy networks, resources and "political entrepreneurs", taking a visionary stance. These are bold proposals, even when they are apparently limited, because they meddle with vested interests, break established routines and challenge the powers that be. And rightly so: realism, the ability to put forward proposals that can be implemented, does not necessarily inhibit the need to think in a way that is completely different.

To give just a few examples: thinking about a new way to manage territorial social and healthcare services, about coastlines and beaches finally freed from the shackles of profiteering and revenue, about traffic laws and regulations that promote slow and sustainable mobility, about a policy capable of finally addressing the issue of housing for the poor, means trying to subvert power relations, lobbies and balances of power that have long been rotting Italy (but also other countries) from the inside and that will be very difficult to dismantle.

This is a primarily cultural endeavour, but one that in turn requires alliances to get off the ground, including those outside the world of universities and research. Without falling into wishful thinking, but at the same time with a healthy dose of determination, the work undertaken with "Ricomporre i divari" proposes a working platform for institutions, but also for any social and economic actors interested in breaking away from established balances and relations of power.

The third element of this common thread is that the vision and concreteness of the proposals can coexist on one condition: the assuming that the issue of inequalities is "the" question around which to develop usable knowledge and research, with a view to establishing a different model of development at the local scale, but also at the multiple global scales. It is due to this that the ecological dimension is so pervasive throughout the book, firmly rooted in the need to turn our gaze to the most fragile people, to their daily lives, to the profound injustices to which they are subjected. Men, women and nature, together, in a different perspective of development.

Through the development and the results of the "Ricomporre i divari" project, it is clearly demonstrated that the issue of the environment truly is a political one. It assumes the centrality of the goal of combating inequalities between regions, territories and cities, but also within cities, and offers a radical reimagining of the model of development under the banner of ecological conversion.

Only if the ecological transition and the fight against inequalities are considered and planned hand in hand can we give the post-pandemic future of cities a solid perspective oriented towards radically rethinking our models of development.

References

Amin A, Thrift N (2016) Seeing like a city. Polity Press, London

Benjaminsen T, Svarstad A (2019) Political ecology. In: Encyclopedia of ecology, vol 4, 2nd edn. Elsevier, Amsterdam, pp 391–396

Brenner N (2004) New state spaces. Oxford University Press, Oxford

Bryant R (ed) (2015) International handbook of political ecology. Edward Elgar, Northampton

Coppola A, Del Fabbro M, Lanzani A, Pessina G, Zanfi F (a cura di) (2021) Ricomporre i divari. Politiche e progetti territoriali contro le disuguaglianze e per la transizione ecologica. Il Mulino, Bologna

Crosta PL, Bianchetti C (2021) Conversazioni sulla ricerca. Donzelli, Roma

De Rossi A (ed) (2018) Riabitare l'Italia. Le aree interne tra abbandoni e riconquiste. Donzelli, Roma

Fainstein S (2011) The just city. Cornell University Press, Ithaca (NY)

Harris Ali H, Keil R (eds) (2008) Networked disease: emerging infections in the global city. Wiley, New York

Latour B (2017) Où atterrir? Comment s'orienter in politique. Le Découverte, Paris

McManus P (2009) Urban political ecology. In: Kitchin R, Thrift N (eds) International encyclopedia of human geography. Elsevier, Amsterdam p, pp 294–303

Mezzadra S, Neilson B (2013) Borders as methods. Duke University Press, Durham

Nietzsche F (2019) The joyous science. Penguin Classics, London

Perreault T, Bridge G, McCarthy J (eds) (2015) Routledge handbook of political ecology. Routledge, London

Pievani T (2020) Finitudine. Un romanzo filosofico su fragilità e libertà. Cortina Editore, Milano

Piketty T (2015) The economics of inequality. Harvard University Press, Cambridge (US)

Piscitelli P (2020) Quando l'aria della città non rende più liberi. Per un'ecologia politica della città. Il lavoro culturale, 3 agosto 2020. https://www.lavoroculturale.org/quando-laria-della-citta-non-rende-piu-liberi/paola-piscitelli/2020/

Quamann D (2012) Spillover. W W Norton & Co Inc., New York

Secchi B (2013) La città dei ricchi e la città dei poveri. Laterza, Bari

Serres M (2001) Hominescence. La Pommier, Paris

Serres M (2009) Temps des crises. La Pommier, Paris

Soja EW (2010) Seeking spatial justice. University of Minnesota Press, Minneapolis

Urry J (2007) Mobilities. Polity Press, London

Chapter 3
Bodies: Propinquity

Abstract The chapter offers a theoretical reflection on how the ongoing pandemics enjoins the need to rethink our proxemics, our everyday ways of coexisting in urban spaces and places. In particular, the chapter proposes the observation of human bodies as the richest point of view for understanding the relations between spaces and practices in urban spaces. Focusing on philosophical literature about touch, the chapter proposes to imagine post-COVID cities as platforms in which different individuals, social groups and populations, characterized by pluralisation of forms of life, can experiment a new life in public, framing distances as a promise of encounter.

3.1 Touch (After COVID)

How will we touch (each other), after all this? How will we exist in proximity to others? How will we inhabit cities and urban space—and in particular, collective spaces—when the most severe phase of the crisis seems behind us, but de facto rules of social distancing, along with our fears, mark out the new boundaries of social interaction in public? How will the scenes of everyday life as a performance, of rituals of interaction, of relations in public play out, when all this has passed?

These are not idle questions. As I leaf through these pages, in December 2021, a new wave of the pandemic is tearing through multiple countries around the world, and further options for the restriction of our autonomy and freedom of movement are currently being considered, after months of relative normality.

Relations in public—to borrow the words of Erving Goffman—are an integral part of urban life, of that "everyday life as performance" that is the way in which we inhabit places and social and spatial relations, the "rituals of interaction" that characterise and constitute them (Goffman 1959, 1963, 1967).

By no means am I proposing to answer these questions in this chapter from the perspective of the designer or the urban planner, nor do I intend to propose operational solutions as regards the use of parks, streets, schools or squares. Many friends and colleagues have done so and continue to do so, and it is a necesary pursuit indeed. I would be happy to merely offer a few reflections on how the ongoing epidemic seems to enjoin the need to rethink our proxemics, our ordinary and everyday ways

G. Pasqui, *Coping with the Pandemic in Fragile Cities*, PoliMI SpringerBriefs,
https://doi.org/10.1007/978-3-030-93979-3_3

of meeting one another and coexisting in urban space. To do this, I have chosen the perspective of a meditation on the sense of touch—a sense that is rather enigmatic in many ways—and of the body (Capitoni 2021).

There were two sources of inspiration for this reflection: a re-reading of Jacques Derrida's *Touching—Jean-Luc Nancy*, (Derrida 2005) and musings upon Cristina Bianchetti's work *Bodies. Between Space and Design* (Bianchetti 2020). Derrida's lengthy text—arduous and baroque though it may often be—goes toe-to-toe with Nancy's entire body of work, making for an extraordinary and powerful meditation on touch, touching and touching oneself in the Western tradition, from Aristotle to phenomenology and beyond. Rereading Nancy's entire oeuvre, Derrida emphasizes how touch constitutes an extraordinary place from which to consider the relationship between the body and the world, but also to test the privilege of sight and the theoretical gaze in the Western tradition.

Bianchetti's work, meanwhile, proved helpful when juxtaposing a reflection on touch and bodies engaged in urban space with critical design thinking, suspicious of any reduction in the complexity of the connections between things and discourses.

When discussing the relationship between the pandemic and urban space from the perspective of architecture and urban planning, there has been no lack of references to the subject of the body. However, as Bianchetti rather effectively shows, we must arm ourselves with a richer way of thinking about the body and its relationship with urban space—a way of thinking that is capable of grasping the inflections and complexity of the dimension of touch. This approach alone can make for an effective guide as we consider the pandemic as a form of living that constrains us whilst at the same time freeing us from traditional forms and cultures of design.

As Bianchetti writes:

> Can urbanism be reformulated on attention to the body? Can the centrality of the *place* be replaced by the place of the body? And is this advantageous? What effects would this have on the regulation of the territory, on major urban issues and how we deal with them? I have tried to identify the ways in which direct or indirect forms of relationship between the body, design and space are established. Ways in which the body has already been the very delicate link between design and the transformation of space. Ways that refer to administrative procedures, to the simplification of codes, to complex dispossession processes, to regulatory frameworks, and to actions that 'touch' the body with the incorporeal of sense as well as with the corporeal of the ground and space, their morphologies, physical infrastructural facilities and economies (Bianchetti 2020: 108).

Working on the link between the body and the city from a post-pandemic perspective therefore means engaging with this complex gaze, for example by carefully reflecting on the dimension of touch.

With this in mind, I would be inclined to start with a very general question. What is the sense of touch? In Western philosophical and scientific thought, the original source of a theory of the five senses is Aristotle's *De Anima* (Aristotle 1984) wherein the Stagirite analyses each of the senses in the context of a general theory of feeling. These are arduous pages indeed: whilst in reference to sight and hearing, for example, Aristotle has no difficulty recognising the "sensorium"—the organ that determines "common sense" or "common sensation" (κοινὴ αἴσθησις)—with regard to touch, he wonders whether the sensorium in question is the flesh or something within the body—under the skin, so to speak. Bringing us to another salient question: what is the place of touch? Is it the skin, with its more or less sensitive sections, with its "areas" and its variable density? Is it the hands, which can brush against one another, touch our own bodies and define their boundaries? Is it the mouth, which suckles at the breast in the first carnal encounter with our mother, which kisses in an experience of maximum closeness, maximum distance? After much uncertainty—related, for example, to the fact that we also perceive other bodies through the layers that exist between us and others, as well as through the prostheses that we use (consider the gloves that we wear to do our shopping at the supermarket)—Aristotle finally seems to reach the conclusion that the flesh is the medium of the tactile faculty. We could therefore reasonably wonder what will become of the flesh of the city, how will this carnal encounter with the space of the city—with the people and things that encumber the urban space—play out, what are we to expect from the new encounters that we will have?

There is no need to highlight that the Western tradition has been constituted based on the prioritisation of sight—sensible and supersensible—as the primary sense, of "theory" as vision. We need only recall the opening of Aristotle's *Metaphysics*, in which he writes that men "take delight in their senses; for even apart from their usefulness they are loved for themselves; and above all others the sense of sight" (*Met.*, 980a). Sight has always been considered the main sense, at once a tool and a metaphor for knowledge, which places things at a distance, which touches with the gaze without physical contact. On the other hand, the eye does not actually touch anything, in the proper sense: I can kiss an eye, but this action has nothing to do with seeing.

And yet, as Aristotle himself does not fail to recognise, touch has a certain primordial nature, because it is the sense we use to make our way through a surrounding space, to piece together a map of possible pathways, aids and obstacles. But also because touch brings into play a two-way relationship between the body and the world: to touch is to be touched. This happens in both a direct form, on the skin, and a mediated form, through an intermediary body. "But there is this difference between the tangible on the one hand and visible and resonant things on the other: the latter we perceive because the medium acts in a certain way upon us, while tangible objects we perceive not by any action upon us of the medium, but concurrently with it, like the man who is struck through his shield" (*De An.*, 423b). So what happens when we become familiar with the city? Which sense, which senses are we putting to work? In what relationship of reciprocity, in what connection/disconnection between our body—the body as *Leib* of the phenomenological tradition—and the "flesh of the world", using Merleau-Ponty vocabulary? How do we touch the city and how do we allow it to pass through us?

3.2   Urban Synaesthesia and the Weight of Our Body

Touch, in how we experience the world, never works alone. It goes hand in hand with other senses (such as taste, as Aristotle already noted), but more than that, our tactile orientation in the world is intertwined with our visual and auditory orientation. As I have observed in the past (Pasqui 2008), our experience of urban space is always profoundly synaesthetic. Even the gaze, which keeps the outside world at a distance in its continuous process of focusing and refocusing, constructing and reconstructing the foreground and background, occurs as part of a complex of sensations that accompany the fine texture of an experience. In the days of the first lockdown, even my view from my window, from my balcony, out towards the city and the street, in the direction of a bypass crossed by a mere handful of cars, the old gasometers cutting a stark figure against the landscape, was made up of silence, of the piercing shriek of the ambulance, of the scent of the blossoms in the tiny garden just outside. Just as the route taken by the number 90 trolleybus, along the ring road, has always been—and always will be the synaesthetic experience par excellence: sounds, smells, contact, rubbing, knocks, lights and shadows, perspectives and vantage points (Briata and Bricocoli Bovo 2018). I feel that it is important to accept the synaesthetic nature of the experience so as to grasp how the new condition of distancing is delivering us not to an anaesthesia, but to new kinds of synaesthesia, to new ways of engaging with space which will be defined based on different interweavings between senses and things, bodies and prostheses.

The reference to the complex nature of the corporeal experience is an allusion to Carlo Sini's work on "bodily graphemes" (Sini 2012). Sini strongly emphasizes the primeval nature of "amodal perception", which is primary as compared with the distinction between the senses, which is always secondary and analytical and as such a product of language (Sini 2012: 81). Our encounter with urban space also presents these amodal and synaesthetic traits which, naturally, when translated into words, are necessarily traced back to analytical distinctions between the senses. Rethinking our sensory encounters with the city therefore entails imagining unprecedented forms of this amodal, synaesthetic texture, but also new words to describe it.

Another aspect to consider. We inhabit the city in the encumbrance and the constriction of our bodies. Encumbrance, because we are forced to carry our bodies around with us without ever being able to free ourselves of them. Constriction, because our bodies define the possibilities and limits of any encounter based on its natural history, which then becomes the life of each body, its encounters, its transformations. Our body is always a perspective, a point of view.

Any encounter with the city is therefore first and foremost a carnal undertaking. Walking along and looking at the wall that marks out the edges of the rail yard, just as you come out onto the street, and catching a glimpse of the backdrop: the skyscrapers near Garibaldi station. Getting on and off the tram. Grazing past people on the pavement. Smelling the exhaust fumes, which irritate your throat. Listening to the birds singing early in the morning in Piazza Leonardo da Vinci. Any encounter with the city—as poetry has taught us in countless ways, both before and after

Baudelaire—is always an encounter between a body and the bodies of others, as well as with the urban body as a whole. Textures, materials, shapes, aids and obstacles. All these elements may change in intensity, but not in nature. We will always inevitably give our body to the world, for example in the form of the urban, the city of stone and the city of men, because the body is nothing more than a fold of the world, a world that continually folds and unfolds itself.

3.3   Prostheses and Distancing

In recent months, every time we have left the house, we have carefully put on a mask to cover our nose and mouth. What is this mask? A self-immunisation device, a filter. A film that separates us whilst at the same time uniting us to the body of the world, the urban body, for example by bringing into focus, drawing our attention to, the act of breathing, a function normally relegated to the background of our active consciousness. However, upon closer examination our bodies have long— always, in fact—been protected by prostheses, by filters. Animal skins or tunics. Armour. Hat, scarf, clothes, shoes. Gloves. But also glasses, hearing aids, nowadays even smartphones which by bringing a monument on which a microchip has been installed into view—frames the work and opens a file which presents it, a magical filter between the eye and the thing. We have always been in a mediated relationship with the urban body, with the body of the world: mediated by prostheses, which have always marked us out as technological animals, protecting us and insulating us—at least to some extent from the dangers of encountering other bodies (Sini 2009). An encounter, an interpenetration—as Spinoza, and with him Deleuze, explains—which can be good or bad (Deleuze 2007). Breathing in poisonous gases? A bad encounter. Walking through a clearing in a vast metropolitan park, perhaps even barefoot? A good encounter.

So what changes in the world of "social distancing"? What and how many new prostheses will we have to wear? How will our relationship with bodies and things be mediated? Working—including in terms of design on prostheses so that we can continue to feel in some way; mapping out new encounters, whether good or bad; calculating conditions of possibility and the limits of proximity: this is what we will undoubtedly do, what we will have to do.

How can we keep our distance? What is the "right distance"? This is an issue inherent to the urban, which has always been, since its origins, a place of inter-mingling and hybridisation. A "bastard" place, perhaps, but one in which forms and practices of distancing and confinement nonetheless establish the very fabric of space. Dividing, for example, the city of the rich from the city of the poor; the city of trade from the city of production; the city of consumption from the city of leisure; the city of movement from the city of stasis. But what kind of distancing can there be without contact? What kind of contact can there be without contagion? Nancy, in his wonderful book *La ville au loin*, wrote that if the city "does not capture itself under an identity, but rather lets itself be touched by paths, traces, outlines", in it "we brush right past one another as we walk by, briefly touching and moving in opposite directions: all in one single movement". Everything that appears in the city, "we touch without touching, and we are touched". If there is contagious contact, "it is the contagion of distance, disseminated communication" (Nancy 1999: 53–59). Distancing and contact, contact and contagion must therefore be considered together, in their mutual relationships. Our urban world will therefore have to reactivate new dances of creating distance, new ways of bringing us closer together and farther away. We are called upon to pay an unprecedented level of attention to the body in its essential distance.

Con-tact, from *cum* and *tangere*: to touch together. How can we imagine a form of con-tact in urban space that limits, inhibits, even precludes touching one another, maintaining a distance, but at the same time connects us, unites us, establishes relationships? In other words, how can we think about spacing? This theme has been a common thread running through the entirety of Jean-Luc Nancy's ontological musings, particularly his meditation on the *co-* (or *cum*) in *Being Singular Plural* (Nancy 2000). This seems to me to be the most important, but also the most critical issue: how can we make the space of the *co-*, the *cum*, visible—that is, spacing as the co-presence and appearance of differences in the city—when the very possibility of touch, of *con*-tact, is precluded? To what extent can this long-distance communication, in open space and collective places, become a promise of some kind of *co*-existence, a form of sharing that shares nothing more than the same spacing, the same distancing? I would posit that what happens and what may yet happen in our encounters in open space, on the pavement, in the streets, the squares, the gardens and parks may not have to be interpreted in a solely defective and privative form. Experiencing what it is to live together, accepting that the *co-*, the "with", is an achievement and a privilege, learning to reduce the distances, within the incommensurable and ineradicable hiatus that both separates and unites us.

I have no way of predicting what will happen to our distances, to our bodies, to how we touch, how we touch one another. We will have to find out for ourselves. Of course, what awaits us is frightening in that it seems to radicalise that movement of self-immunisation, of distancing that our technological prostheses had already exacerbated. Worse still, what promises to befall us could, at least in part, restrict the space of touch, of the embrace, of the caress, to within the confines of our homes, sterilising the tactile dimension of the urban encounter in that collective space about which Baudelaire waxed lyrical, which Simmel described so extraordinarily, seeming to connote the idea of the city that we have developed over the centuries. In light of this, we will have to imagine and design spaces capable of ensuring the proper distances, but also of conveying a new means of bringing us closer together, a new proxemics that addresses the issue of this distance and, within this very distance, focuses on our bodies, their relationships, and their opportunities to encounter one another. Making the city the place in which we can experiment with a new life in public: one which can slow its pace, which makes opportunities for closeness a focal point, which frames distance as a promise of encounter, the touch of our gaze, of our breath.

Perhaps our nostalgia for the proximity of bodies, of the crowd, of demonstrations, of concerts in public squares or parks will linger for a while. It is certainly a nostalgia that I feel keenly. But I also think about the innate ambivalence of that crowd, of those bodies. Density is not always a choice; often, it is the mark of poverty, of fragile housing or social circumstances. So start by taking a more careful look around you; pay attention to gestures, bodies, and movements. Perhaps for today, this is all we can do: endeavour to pay closer attention, to care for our bodies, our space, and the connections between them—a care that could open up new avenues to us, including new ways of rethinking the post-pandemic city.

References

Aristotle (1984) Complete works of Aristotle. Princeton University Press, Princeton
Bianchetti C (2020) Bodies: between space and design. Jovis, Barcelona
Briata P, Bricocoli Bovo M (2018) Diversity on board: the 90/91 trolley-bus in Milan as a "cosmopolitan canopy". Paper presented at 2018 AESOP conference
Capitoni F (2021) Toccare. Jaca Book, Milano
Deleuze G. (2007) Cosa può un corpo? Lezioni su Spinoza. Ombre Corte, Verona
Derrida J (2005) On touching. Jean-Luc Nancy. Stanford University Press, Stanford
Goffman E (1959) The presentation of self in everyday life. Anchor Books, New York
Goffman E (1963) Behaviour in public places. Free Press, New York
Goffman E (1967) Interaction ritual: essays on face-to-face behavior. Anchor Books, New York
Nancy J-L (2000) Being singular plural. Stanford University Press, Stanford
Nancy J-L (1999) La ville au loin. La Prochide, Paris
Pasqui G (2008) Città, popolazioni, politiche. Jaca Book, Milano
Sini C (2009) Ethics of writings. SUNY Press, Albany (NY)
Sini C (2012) Il sapere dei segni. Jaca Book, Milano

Chapter 4
Cities: Space/Time

Abstract The starting point of this chapter is the concept of urban rhythm as the key to understand the consequences and effects of urban space–time dynamics after pandemic. Critically analysing the international literature about the urban effects of pandemic, the chapter discusses the most relevant consequences of COVID-19 on supply and value chains, mobility, labour organisation restructuring connected with the raising of remote working. In the last part of the chapter the case of Milan is presented, with particular attention to the "15-min strategy" proposed by Milan Municipality in June 2020.

4.1 Time and Rhythms

During the most severe phase of the pandemic, we experienced the suspension of the traditional connection between spaces and rhythms in the urban sphere. We know that cities are a palimpsest (Corboz 1983), and that this palimpsest in inscribed in a multitude of urban rhythms that depend upon the coexistence of populations, practices, localised interactions, regular and irregular movements (Pasqui 2016).

In a 1991 essay that proved to be remarkably prescient of much of the more recent (and often repetitive) literature on our fluid and flexible modernity, Alberto Melucci founded his reflections upon the radical transformations of the figures of time in the contemporary world, as well as on the contradiction between linear social time and the "multiple and discontinuous" time of the subjective experience (Melucci 1996). The former is characterised by the continuity and uniqueness of events, which occur in succession in one direction only, thus proving irreversible. The latter, meanwhile, is both cyclical and simultaneous; it is the time of our everyday experiences, characterised by its variable rhythms.

What we saw in the cities during the pandemic was the interaction between these two times being redefined, as a consequence of a phenomenon of rarefaction and concentration of activities. Rarefaction, because our cities shut down completely for varying lengths of time, reducing the movement of urban populations that has always characterised them (Pasqui 2016). Concentration, because a single place (our homes

G. Pasqui, *Coping with the Pandemic in Fragile Cities*, PoliMI SpringerBriefs,
https://doi.org/10.1007/978-3-030-93979-3_4

and their internal spaces) became the location where a multitude of activities and practices—which normally took place in different parts of the city—now overlapped.

So how can we consider the time/space of the city during and after the pandemic? The first step that I propose is to reconceptualise the urban and its populations, starting with the notion of rhythm. Indeed, the temporality of the city that experiences the oscillation to which Melucci refers can be connoted first and foremost by *rhythm*. By rhythm, I mean the very condition of possibility inherent to linear, chronological time. As the philosopher Carlo Sini writes: "Time can only emerge as a measure of distance through rhythm. Distance has and already is in itself rhythm, and it is here that time quite literally exists and finds space" (Sini 1989: 82).

What is rhythmic? The trajectories of movement of a vast number of populations: not only commuters, but also those who only live in the city for certain sections of the day or for certain periods of the week, month or year. What is rhythmic? The systolic and diastolic movement that characterises the breathing of the city: because the city breathes, and it is this breath that provides the conditions of possibility for the rhythm of the various populations that inhabit it, that pass through it. What is rhythmic? The very organisation of activities and functions, which in turn influence the structure itself of our urban spaces.

What happened during the pandemic? The spaces/times of the city redefined their rhythms by activating systems to control and reduce mobility, by reorganising productive and commercial activities, by changing the behaviours of urban populations.

In order to gain an idea of what has happened and to think about the possible future, it would be wise to start from the observation that when we describe a population, we are faced with its rhythm, but also the way in which this rhythm corresponds to the rhythm of the city, in its organisation over the course of the day, the month, the year—over life as a whole.

The rhythm of people, together with the rhythm of the city, weave a fabric of continuity in their peculiar polyrhythm. Within this fabric, however, change also occurs: a change that takes place in the weft of its practices, rewriting them as new practices and continually redefining them.

So how does this disruption within the rhythm of practices occur? How can changes take place in everyday life? If we observe urban populations, we can clearly see the 'interplay' between difference and repetition in action.

As we sought to demonstrate in Chap. 2, any practice is always the interweaving of many different practices. Its event (its "occasion") is a transit, a flow, within which subjects and objects are constituted (and regenerated). This transit is continuous, and this continuity is also provided by the polyrhythmic interweaving that characterises them.

Change can, of course, take place in many different ways, but it is clear that in the weft and concatenation of practices, it takes the form of a progressive accumulation of tiny shifts. New uses for old functions, when they arise, are not necessarily perceived as such—they are not always planned; indeed, in most cases they come about unconsciously and regardless of any intentions.

The shift within the weft of practices happens because the occurrence of each practice is at once a repetition (any practice is always the socially determined reproduction of other similar practices) and a difference (even if this is merely the imperceptible distinction that repetition itself generates). Difference within repetition, repetition as difference.

Change takes place within the rhythm of practices, in the form of the imperceptible shift of one practice into another within a constant oscillation between difference and repetition.

As such, we cannot honestly describe cities during and after the pandemic as entirely different places. Rhythms and times/spaces change in relation to continuous shifts, and it is these shifts that we must consider, despite the fact that the stark fracture represented by the lockdown has apparently alluded to a sudden and radical mutation.

Every shift, every change in how the city is used brings about a transformation in its peculiar "polyrhythm". Just consider the changes in the rhythm of consumer activities, generated both by the limited access to shops and shopping centres and by the galloping development of online shopping. In much the same vein, it is worth reflecting on the rhythm imposed by the pandemic on the use of outdoor spaces (parks, gardens, streets and squares) as well as the consequences, which we will subsequently consider in greater depth, on remote learning and working.

Typically, the polyrhythm of the city also implies a link between the movement, speed and temporality of its people. The spatialisation of the flows of urban populations is not merely a question of densifications, of clumps formed by establishing places (either permanent or temporary) in which social practices (of work, care, consumption, entertainment, but also waiting and movement itself) are structured in space.

It is also a question of speed and intensity. The speed of the movements, the intensity of the flows, which are in turn intertwined with the nature of the practices.

Ultimately, as previously mentioned, we have a lot to deal with: (not only) time, but also (perhaps above all) rhythms. The rhythms of daily or weekly routines, the rhythms of work and care, the rhythms of the body (our own and that of the world).

It is precisely these rhythms that have been subjected to strong torsion, gradually adapting to, for example, the intensive use for those lucky enough to have them available of holiday homes as stable workplaces, with significant changes to the rhythm of their daily and weekly movements.

During the first phase of the pandemic, when we observed people within the flows of the practices that make up life, what we discovered was that it is the dance of the rhythm that matters—the downbeat and upbeat of everyday life—which is irreducible to linear time.

The everyday life of the city, the practices of using urban space, the variably constrained forms of mobility that gave us new rhythms that are also new spaces, and spaces that are in turn speeds and intensities of movement. The rhythm of children or the elderly; the rhythm of foreigners; the rhythm of young people on weekend nights; the rhythm of new jobs (consider the incessant movement of raiders in big cities):

all these rhythms mark the space, distort it (as evidenced by lengthened or shortened maps which measure distances in travel times), thicken and thin it in relation to their varying intensities.

4.2   Urban Effects

Based on this representation of the city as a weft and palimpsest of spatio-temporal relationships and processes characterised by overlapping rhythms, we can start to reflect upon the urban effects of the pandemic. I am referring not to the effects that are guests of the city, but rather to the effects that have a direct impact on the organisation and practices of use of the urban space. In order to recognise these types of effects, I believe that it is very important to start from the practices—from what people, companies and institutions do—with a particular focus on recognising the effects in everyday life.

As part of the survey conducted on behalf of the FEEM Foundation and written up in Bandarin et al. (2021), a global Delphi survey of 20 cities was conducted in the middle of 2020 which clearly evidences the key aspects of the short-term urban impact of the pandemic and the respondents' expectations in terms of its longer-term effects.

In essence, the survey first of all underlines the possible connection between job restructuring and increasing inequalities. Secondly, it casts light on the outcomes in terms of the increased weighting towards the Internet in social interaction practices, at the expense of in-person events, along with the consequent impoverishment of public life. Thirdly, from a structural point of view, the survey highlights the centrality of the issue of housing: a problem exacerbated by the growing pressure resulting from the intensive and often inappropriate use of domestic spaces.

Another economic element of great interest brought up by the survey is that:

> The world is becoming more 'regional'. In particular, production chains will be shorter, the economies will rediscover proximity and nearby places, and local governance will take a more significant role. These processes are already taking place, and a partial reshoring of production is underway (Bandarin et al. 2021: 3).

When viewed together, these expected effects paint a picture of a set of impacts at a global scale and processes of differentiated socio-spatial reorganisation at the scale of individual cities. Amongst the most significant dimensions of this reorganisation, I would especially like to mention the following points.

A first important dimension is that related to production. Where, how, in which territories and within which supply chains and value chains did production continue over the course of 2020 and 2021? And which sectors instead lagged behind? What effects will we see on the business system, on the balances struck between different drivers of the urban economy in the various cities across Italy, which are characterised by highly diversified urban economic foundations? According to the Bank of Italy's analysis of the Italian economy in 2020, the manufacturing sector generally maintained its usual course, whilst certain service sectors that were previously seeing excellent growth (first and foremost tourism) took a major hit (Bank of Italy 2021). The consequences on the urban model of development (consider, over the years immediately preceding the pandemic, how Airbnb exploded, taking precedence over new low-cost chains in the tourist accommodation sector) must, of course, be assessed in great detail, including in relation to their potential effects on the property market (Nomisma 2020).

This is a market that has slowed down considerably in Italy—with just a few exceptions, including Milan—since the first few months following the start of the first wave of the pandemic, especially in terms of the volume of sales, and even after signs of recovery over the summer of 2020, no significant recovery will truly pick up steam until 2022.

From the point of view of consumption, in the most central urban environments, the pandemic has catalysed the radicalisation of certain phenomena that were already underway: the development of online shopping and the reorganisation of local trade. The two phenomena, which go hand in hand with one another, provide an insight into the potential crisis of the large-scale retail sector which, especially in larger urban areas, could result in significant displacement effects, with disused commercial spaces requiring rethinking and redesign.

Another element that is both structural and strongly linked to everyday life is related to mobility practices. The data collected over the course of 2020 in Italian cities highlights some significant elements regarding the shifts in public and private mobility practices, both fast and slow. Whilst during the first lockdown, commuting between home and work as well as occasional trips fell substantially, over the subsequent period, the restrictions in place seem to have affected occasional trips more severely. The radical change in habits therefore resulted in the need to stay at home being more keenly perceived and strictly observed, limiting even occasional travel.

What's more, the perception of public transportation being unsafe to use led to an increase in the use of non-polluting means of transport (from bicycles to scooters), but also a return to the use of the car as a private means of transport.

Here, again, it is difficult to imagine to what extent this will remain as a long-term effect once the dust has settled, both in terms of individual choices—and therefore the demand for different types of vehicles—and in terms of the public and private mobility on offer. Nonetheless, the issue of the urban ecological transition—also understood as a radical reduction in the use of cars in the city—is very much the matter at hand here.

Ultimately, people in Italian cities produced (and worked) differently, moving around much less. This had led to an increased focus on housing issues, on the deep-seated differences between how the better-off and the worse-off in society live, but also on the presence of both private and collective outdoor areas within residential spaces (communal gardens, courtyards, terraces, even rooftops). In addition, spending more time at home and thus near our homes highlighted how fundamental it is to have both public and private services in the neighbourhood: the concept of the so-called "15-min city" which we will return to shortly.

A renewed interest in our living situations has brought to the fore how the issue of housing for all, and especially housing for the poor, but also the living conditions in neighbourhoods, the maintenance of collective and public spaces, the accessibility of services, is now establishing a new geography of critical areas, presenting serious structural problems for public action to resolve.

In the previous chapter, I already touched upon another issue that I consider to be relevant, namely: what will happen to life in public, to social interaction spatialised in places? I have no way of predicting what will happen to our distances, to our bodies, to how we touch, how we touch one another. We will have to find out for ourselves, and a great deal will depend upon the future dynamics of this and (unfortunately) perhaps other pandemics. Of course, what awaits us is frightening in that it seems to radicalise that movement of self-immunisation, of distancing that was already a prominent feature of our cities. In light of this, we will have to imagine and design spaces capable of ensuring the proper distances, but also of conveying a new means of bringing us closer together, a new proxemics that addresses the issue of this distance and, within this very distance, focuses on our bodies, their relationships, and their opportunities to encounter one another. Making the city the place in which we can experiment with a new life in public.

Within this general framework, I would like to devote some space to what I consider to be the most pervasive consequence of the pandemic, which is perhaps set to become a permanent and structural aspect of our lives: the extension of remote working, especially in the service sector (banks, insurance companies, business services, but also the liberal professions, from architecture studios and engineering firms to accountants, from lawyers to marketing and communication agencies), which is so central to the urban economy of many Italian cities.

The survey conducted on behalf of the FEEM Foundation (2021) shows that, on a global scale, the impact of the spread of working from home on urban spaces is considered to be incredibly significant, having become a feature of around 40% of all non-manual jobs. As regards Milan itself, at an event ("Your Next Milano") promoted by Assolombarda and Milano & Partners at the end of 2020, the data from a survey was presented according to which, once the pandemic is behind us, the use of remote working in Milan will be markedly more widespread than in the past, with company projections suggesting that it will be used by 75% of industrial companies and business services firms in the city of Milan (as opposed to 43% before the crisis) and 54% in the metropolitan area (up from 20%).

Of course, the figure regarding Milan depends on the specific composition of economic activities found in that city: however, it seems to me to be indicative of a process that may take on a structural nature in relation to company reorganisation processes. Indeed, many other cities across Italy and Europe were shown to have similar dynamics.

So what are we seeing in terms of the spatial effects of remote working? I believe that there are three essential dimensions at work here. The first concerns possible changes to the distribution between modes of transport (public/private; individual/collective) and the demand for public mobility. This aspect plays a central role in the design of more eco-friendly cities and opens the door to a profound rethinking of the role and management of public transportation at the urban and regional scales.

The second dimension has to do with the possible displacement effects on property operations concentrating on business services (banks and insurance companies, IT services, consultancy) and on the professions, with possible impacts in terms of new divestment and with a need to reinvent the flexible use of spaces that are often characterised by extreme rigidity of use (consider the towering office blocks in areas of urban transformation, which were desolately empty and abandoned for months in many cities across Europe).

Finally, the third relates to the effects on the demand for new collective workspaces, characterised by the growing demand for digital infrastructure. The research currently underway on this issue (Mariotti and Akhavan 2020) shows that the very notion of coworking should be redefined in light of a major extension and resignification of collective work.

Each of these consequences brings into play significant spatial and social structures, requiring a rethinking of the urban development model, which must also find a stable foothold in public policies.

4.3 An Example: Milan

Over the years, I have had the opportunity to more closely examine my city, Milan, taking as a reference not only the municipality, but also the territory of the metropolitan area, and I would like to illustrate what form the effects of the pandemic crisis are taking in the Milan urban region.

An initial question concerns the effects on the business system, on the balances between the various drivers of the urban economy in the Milan region. According to the first findings and forecasts (for example those proposed by Assolombarda, including on the basis of the economic analyses performed by REF Ricerche), after the collapse seen in the first half of 2020, the economy of Lombardy and Milan has shown some recovery (even though there was an approximately 10% drop in Lombardy's GDP in 2020). However, these dynamics are not uniform.

I have already mentioned the possible effects on the reorganisation of non-manual work in the context of Milan. In certain highly specialised sectors (banking, insurance, high value-added services to businesses, publishing), the spatial outcome of the mass shift to remote working may lead to phenomena of partial divestment, the management of which will require a bold and imaginative approach in terms of design. The alienating effect of these towering office blocks falling silent as they were abandoned during the first lockdown, even in the vast new developments of Porta Nuova and City Life, shows that the question of how to repurpose office workspaces will undoubtedly be one of the key issues of urban redesign over the coming years.

In terms of property, however, Milan has not only sustained, but even accelerated certain dynamics that were previously underway. In its comparative analysis of sales of residential and commercial buildings between March 2019 and March

2020, the National Council of Notaries recorded a drop of -55.4% and -59.3% (respectively) in Milan. Despite this decline in sales, the average prices ($€5700/m^2$) actually increased by $+1.8\%$.

In the Lombardy capital, the average price varies substantially depending on which urban macro-area we consider: in the centre, it ranges from $€8500$ to $€10,200$ per m^2, with highs of up to $€16,300$; meanwhile, in semi-central areas it is between $€4250$ and $€5580$, with peripheral areas trailing behind at $€3280–€3950$.

These figures should also be considered together with the fact that with very few exceptions (Westfield's large-scale retail investment in Segrate), any major property operations already underway did not stop. Quite the contrary: construction was one of the first sectors to get back into full swing after the first lockdown.

The city's excellent international reputation explains the completion of the major urban transformations that had been started, perhaps most notably the MIND project headed up by Australian developer Lendlease in the EXPO area, which, in June 2020, as soon as the lockdown was lifted, confirmed all its investments by presenting the design for the first operation phase, whilst work continues on the Human Technopole Research Laboratories and the Galeazzi Hospital. At the same time, Milanese developer COIMA is also completing its Gioia 22 complex as well as continuing work on a series of other operations, such as those underway on the city's main former railway yards.

From the point of view of consumption, in the most central urban environment, the pandemic has catalysed the radicalisation of certain phenomena that were already underway: the development of online shopping and the reorganisation of local trade.

Another element that is both structural and strongly linked to everyday life is related to mobility practices. The data collected over the course of 2020 highlights some significant elements regarding the shifts in public and private mobility practices, both fast and slow.

The data provided by AMAT (Milan's Agency for Mobility, the Environment and the Territory), for example, highlighted how the measures taken to contain the contagion initially brought about a significant and progressive reduction in travel in the city of Milan.

According to the information reported by AMAT in its "Issues paper on the variation of indicators relating to the mobility systems in Milan in the wake of the COVID-19 emergency", monitoring of the number of vehicles passing through the electronic gates of Area B—which corresponds to most of the territory of the city of Milan—showed that there was a considerable drop in traffic in the first half of 2020, with daily peaks of up to -77%. On average, the reduction was -55%.

Whilst during the first lockdown, commuting between home and work as well as occasional trips both fell by around 25%, over the second lockdown, the "stay at home" messaging and associated restrictions seem to have affected occasional trips more severely.

What's more, as we shall see in the next chapter, the effects in terms of growth of inequality were not evenly distributed across the city. The peripheral areas—both those located farther from the historical centre and the enclaves closer to the central area—suffered the heaviest social and economic effects.

In this context, in April 2020 the City of Milan published a document entitled "Milan 2020: Adaptation Strategy", in which it attempted to lay out a strategy for the city's recovery following the health crisis, launching various immediate or planned actions for managing a "new normality" (Comune di Milano 2020). The document, which was open to comments and contributions from the entire city, represented the city administration's platform for reflection over the course of 2020, adopting as its core principle an approach already taken by other European cities, namely to bolster public services with a view to creating proximity, mainly by ensuring access to them within a 15-min walk, redressing the balance between unequal neighbourhoods, promoting specific features and seeking to reduce the need for travel between neighbourhoods.

More generally, the document emphatically reaffirms the idea of urban rhythms and times, but also the need to take a sustainable approach to urban regeneration in order to build strategies for resilience.

The document certainly makes for interesting reading, although one could argue that the 15-min city already exists in Milan: specifically, it is the dense city located within the outer ring road, where the levels of not just services, but also income and human and social capital, are much higher. A plan capable of guaranteeing access to similar facilities and services not only on the outskirts of the city, but also in the wider context of the metropolitan area.

In my opinion, this implies a radical change in the model of development, with real engagement with the ideas of preparedness (Balducci 2020) and resilience. An urban ecological transition requires some very strong decisions: environmental issues necessarily call for a rearrangement of priorities and powers (Bryant 2015), but also a focus on the redistributive effects of policies and investments.

In Milan, as in many other European cities, the next few years will represent a unique opportunity to redefine the urban development model with an environmental focus, not least due to the huge amount of resources for investments that will be earmarked for urban areas as part of the 2021/2027 plan for structural funds and the National Plan for Recovery and Resilience.

In this context, I can discern three priorities for a new phase of urban policies for Milan, centred around the themes of combating inequalities and bringing about an environmental conversion.

The first priority is to support the conversion of urban economies to make them more environmentally friendly, using measures capable—in the various situations and contexts involved of promoting the revival of local economies and the reorientation of products, processes and supply chains. This conversion may be implemented both in sectors such as tourism and in manufacturing supply chains, using energy efficiency and saving processes, experiments in terms of logistics and freight transport, and product innovations with a view to reuse and recycle. In this context, another crucial aspect is the support for urban and territorial policies aimed at increasing resilience against climate change by means of innovation across the board: of the energy technologies employed in construction, of public and private mobility, of the redevelopment of blue and green infrastructures—including with a view to combating hydrogeological fragility—of the regeneration of disused or underused assets, doing everything possible to avoid further consumption of undeveloped land.

On the other hand, perhaps this is the right time to put in place an overarching urban plan for the exceptional maintenance of our material welfare, which would consist of various ingredients: small projects that would also have the advantage of being quick to implement, upgrading the energy infrastructure of the building stock, especially where it is linked to the offer of rent-controlled housing or social housing, redesigning the urban land to make it more permeable to water, reduce the incidence of heat island phenomena and open it up to use by different social actors, and promoting infrastructure for slow mobility and cycling.

This means equipping ourselves with an integrated policy for the redevelopment and regeneration of the public assets of our so-called material welfare and, more extensively, of the infrastructures of the "fundamental economy" (houses, schools, health centres, sports facilities, other territorial services, parks and green areas, but also roads, sewers, basic commercial structures), through support for integrated local projects that utilise these assets as a tool for social integration and environmental and ecological redevelopment. A policy of this kind would use welfare centres as territorial hubs on which to build veritable "local contracts" involving institutions, civil society organisations, active citizens and companies.

This sort of approach, which engages not only with space, but also time and rhythms, would necessarily require some orientation in terms of implementation, which would also entail a radical overhaul in terms of administration management.

As already pointed out in the document produced by the City of Milan, it is crucial to immediately start rolling out experimental, reversible actions that can test out a variety of tools and solutions.

Secondly, it is important to always bear in mind the real-world effects on everyday life of any actions, projects and initiatives, from a perspective that is attentive to the materiality of the relationship between forms of space and ordinary practices. This means having an accurate understanding of how aspects such as the organisation of work, mobility, schools, and the use of parks and open spaces actually work. This close-to-practice, experiential approach must incorporate analytical evidence, data and models with a view to building solutions deemed plausible and credible for those who have to implement and interact with them in everyday life.

Thirdly, it is important to work on the city's ability to prepare itself by designing territorial networks not only in terms of social and healthcare, but also with regard to mobility, forms of labour and services. In order to do this, it is also essential to work on people and families, helping to empower them with regard to the conditions of the ongoing emergency and the effects of the economic crisis that is already affecting the lives and futures of the most vulnerable in society. Furthermore, this means engaging the involvement of the social forces, intermediate bodies, and networks of associations and volunteers that have mobilised in recent months as a resource rather than an obstacle, because the complexity of the processes at work is an extraordinary resource for collective learning, legitimisation and effectiveness when it comes to their implementation.

These principles need to be concretely tested out in complex, multi-actor processes which prioritise the most critical areas and the urban and metropolitan peripheries. Under these conditions, policies introduced to combat the dramatic effects of the pandemic can offer a decisive turning point for rethinking Milan's urban development with a marked emphasis on socio-spatial justice and an environmental conversion.

References

Balducci A (2020) Planning for resilience. In Balducci A, Chiffi D, Curci F (eds) Risk and resilience. Springer Brief, Berlin-Milano, pp 15–25

Bank of Italy (2021) Bollettino economico, n.1, March

Bandarin F, Ciciotti E, Cremaschi M, Madera G, Perulli P. Shendikova D (2021) After Covid-19: a survey on the prospects for cities. City, Culture, Society, in press

Bryant R (ed) (2015) International Handbook of Political Ecology. Edward Elgar, Northampton

Comune di Milano (2020) Milano 2020. Strategie di adattamento, April divari. Politiche e progetti territoriali contro le disuguaglianze e per la transizione ecologica. Il Mulino, Bologna

Corboz P (1983) The land as a palimpsest. Diogenes 31:12–34

FEEM (2020) Which future for cities after Covid-19. An international survey, Fondazione "Enrico Mattei", October

Mariotti I, Akhavan M (2020) Exploring proximities in coworking spaces: evidence from Italy. Eur Spatial Res Policy 27(1):37–52

Melucci A (1996) The playing self. Cambridge University Press, Cambridge (UK)

Nomisma (2020) Terzo Rapporto sul mercato immobiliare 2020. Bologna, December

Pasqui G (2016) Populations and rhythms in contemporary cities. In: Pucci P, Colleoni M (eds) Understanding mobilities for designing contemporary cities. Springer, Berlin, pp 49–63

Sini C (1989) La storia, il tempo e la parola. In Il silenzio e la parola. Luoghi e confini del sapere per un uomo planetario. Marietti, Genova, pp 73–97

Chapter 5
Inequalities: Peripheries

Abstract The social and spatial effects of the dramatic COVID-19 crisis have affected the peripheral areas of Italian and European cities, where is concentrated a significant segment of fragile populations. From this perspective COVID-19 pandemic has been not the cause, but an accelerator of demographic, socio-economic and physical processes that were already underway in the previous years. The chapter explores the effects of pandemic on Italian peripheries, with particular attention to the growing socio-spatial polarisation. In the last part of the chapter the analysis is focused on Milan peripheries.

5.1 A Problem of Socio-spatial Justice

What lasting effects will the dramatic COVID-19 crisis leave on the urban peripheries of Italy's cities? To what extent will the inevitable impacts of the pandemic on the economy and society, but also on cultures and collective imaginations, determine the fate of those who live in the most critical areas of our cities? How should public policies address these effects, and through what mechanisms can they intervene effectively?

Before venturing to offer any answers—which would be wholly provisional, given the overwhelming uncertainty in which we find ourselves, precluding the possibility of establishing any remedies—I would like to point out that the effects of the epidemic are already taking a particular and often dramatic form in our peripheral areas. A significant segment of the fragile population is concentrated in these urban peripheries: some have lost an already precarious job, whilst others risk falling prey to structural unemployment. For obvious reasons, precarious employment is the first victim of the current crisis, and for individuals and families, losing a job—however precarious it may be—often constitutes a first step into a vicious cycle which generally comes to affect their housing situation further down the line. Jobless and homeless: this is the condition in which many families, but also a vast number of individuals (consider, for example, all the young immigrants employed in the less protected, lower added-value service sector up to now), could find themselves within just a few months after the discontinuation of the extraordinary measures put in place for 2020 and part of 2021.

The other dimension in which the difference between richer areas and peripheral or marginal areas is already clearly discernible is that of education and schools. The drastic transition to distance learning proved much less straightforward in schools—especially primary and lower secondary schools—with lower levels of social and cultural capital, but also inferior technological equipment. Foreign children and teenagers who had recently arrived in Italy and who do not speak the language well, along with families unable to guarantee sufficient coverage in terms of connectivity for the few devices they have available to them, were amongst the worst affected by the pandemic in this regard; what's more, schools with more limited technological equipment will also face a great deal of backlash further down the line in terms of an increase in school dropouts, difficulties catching up for students unable to keep up with distance learning activities, and further marginalisation and downgrading of certain schools.

Finally, we must not lose sight of the risks in terms of the regular maintenance of the housing stock, public and welfare services, collective spaces etc., which could suffer from issues of outright abandonment, with their deterioration in material terms easily giving way to an impoverishment of the social relations they facilitate.

How can we tackle these problems? The first step is to reinterpret the very notion of what constitutes an urban periphery, in a way capable of accurately identifying the places and contexts where public action should be most keenly focused.

5.2 Which Peripheries? Which Inequalities?

In a report from the Inequality and Diversity Forum entitled "15 Proposals for Social Justice", produced before the pandemic, the issue of urban peripheries is addressed in the wider context of territorial inequalities (Inequality and Diversity Forum 2019). As extensively documented by the report itself, and more generally by the materials produced and collected by the Forum, territorial inequalities have increased over recent decades throughout the Western world (Piketty 2015) and especially in Europe (Iammarino et al. 2017; European Commission 2017) and Italy, with relevant social and political consequences (Rodríguez-Pose 2017). Reflecting on the relationship between the conditions of peripheries and the growth of inequalities means first of all placing the issue in the context of the growing disparities between different regions and areas of the country. As the report states:

> At the territorial level, the situation in Italy is particularly serious: because of the size of the disparities between regions (for example, the average monthly disposable income in Lombardy is 69% higher than in Calabria), and because all regions across Italy have fallen behind as compared with the rest of Europe. For example, between 2003 and 2017, Lombardy went from 28th to 52nd place in the ranking of European regions by GDP per capita, whilst Emilia-Romagna went from 45th to 72nd (Inequality and Diversity Forum 2019:19).

If urban peripheral areas are places characterised by growing inequalities, what are we really referring to when we talk about peripheries? As Agostino Petrillo has shown (Petrillo 2018, 2020), the notion of "periphery", along with the demarcation of peripheral areas, constitutes a complex research problem in itself. From this perspective, the recent attempts made in Italy to determine the minimum territorial units of investigation and to statistically represent the territorial forms of socio-economic inequality in urban areas allow us to cast light on some important analytical and interpretative problems.

We are not in a position to discuss these attempts in any detail in this volume, so we will instead briefly analyse the results of two key projects, undertaken by the Department for Cohesion Policies (Assessment and Analysis for Planning Unit) and the ISTAT (the Italian Institute of Statistics), respectively, both of which were published in 2017.

The Department drew up poverty maps identifying sub-areas or districts of concentrated deprivation in each of the fourteen Italian metropolitan areas recognised by the Italian legislation. This makes it possible to classify and characterise their features, subsequently providing an operational tool to support urban policies and local planning (Department for Cohesion Policies 2017).

The ISTAT, on the basis of a request from the Parliamentary Commission of Inquiry on the conditions of safety and state of deterioration of cities and their peripheries (Camera dei Deputati 2018), produced and calculated an indicator of social and material vulnerability for the fourteen municipalities identified. The indicator was created by combining various different indicators and aims to produce a standardised, geo-referenced representation of inequalities in the urban environment by using analytical cartograms providing an overview of the situation (ISTAT 2017).

Despite the significant differences between the two projects, the two reports endeavoured first of all to identify the smallest relevant territorial unit for consideration, and secondly to produce concise, multidimensional indicators capable of identifying and representing the territorial morphology of deprivation in a systematic way.

The Department for Cohesion Policies adopted the neighbourhood as its reference unit for this purpose, although the authors of the report openly acknowledge that there is no clear theoretical or statistical definition of the term. From this perspective, the use of a minimum territorial proxy for the neighbourhood based on ISTAT census areas presents us with a problem that is interesting to consider. Based on this and other methodological decisions, these poverty maps paint a picture of the neighbourhoods in question, classified by level and type of deprivation.

The ISTAT report, on the other hand, incorporates a variety of functional subsets which are not always comparable and which differ between the various cities under examination, piecing together summarised values for these areas based on a multi-dimensional battery of indicators calculated by drawing from multiple statistical sources.

Both contributions are extremely important, in that they allow us to base our reflections on accurate, comparable data and to define the different variable at work with suitable precision. Moreover, they both adhere to certain guiding principles which also reveal an implicit theory of the nature of the inequalities concentrated spatially in urban areas. In summary, the guiding principles seem to be:

- financial poverty (be it absolute or relative) is intimately linked to housing poverty, and thus plays a central role in determining the conditions of spatial concentration of the families and individuals living in conditions of economic inequality;
- these inequalities, concentrated in certain parts of cities, are a multidimensional phenomenon contributed to by factors such as social vulnerability—linked to employment conditions—the level and quality of education (and training in a broader sense), accessibility to services, and potential for mobility;
- the deterioration of buildings and the associated fragility of living conditions provide a good approximation for the environmental variables that characterise the most deprived neighbourhoods and areas.

The reports by the Department for Cohesion Policies and the ISTAT each concentrate on non-comparable phenomena (poverty in the former; vulnerability in the latter), non-uniform units of analysis and dissimilar contexts, but they nonetheless offer a very helpful springboard for reflection and discussion on the typical spaces where inequalities are rife in Italian peripheries.

The headline results of the two investigations show a complex geography of peripheries in major urban areas across Italy, but also the continued existence of critical areas, concentrated in some of the largest social housing districts built in the twentieth century and in certain run-down historical neighbourhoods.

After a year and a half of the crisis sparked by the pandemic, we absolutely must check up on the situation in the areas identified by these analyses: never before have we needed an up-to-date geography of socio-spatial inequalities and fragilities.

5.3   History and Places Matter

This up-to-date analysis has to take into account not only the quantitative dimensions of the situation, but also the qualitative ones. As such, I would propose a few additions to the approach described in the previous paragraph.

The first of these concerns the strongly historical dimension of the dynamics of inequality. Over the decades, Italian cities have redrawn the geography of their peripheries time and time again, in response to demographic, social and territorial processes which should be examined in more detail if we are to grasp the historical dimension of the phenomena at work.

The peripheries of metropolitan areas across Europe have long been places characterised by a certain distance and separation (both physical and symbolic) from the centre, but they are also environments in which highly innovative planning, design and policies have been experimented with (Secchi 2005). Over the last quarter of a century, the geography of peripheries has changed radically in line with the collapse of traditional processes of urbanisation.

There are certain characteristics of this change which should, of course, be specifically adapted to each individual urban area in the country and interpreted along with the material and symbolic evolution of urban forms (Balducci et al. 2017). Furthermore, these processes are deeply linked to each area's history, which has led to phenomena such as a structural crisis and a reduction in levels of material and immaterial wellbeing.

The first feature of these dynamics is the extremely strong connection between demographic change and peripheral conditions. The two processes that characterise Italy's demographic dynamics are concentrated in the peripheries, namely the ageing of the Italian population (often the result of the continued presence of families who have now grown older in public housing districts) and the substantial presence of immigrant populations (both legal and illegal). The demographic dynamics in peripheral areas are too important to be overlooked. Many of the historical peripheries of Italian cities started life as uniform settlements intended to house urban working families, who often had stable employment conditions and expectations of improving their social and economic status. Nowadays, it is precisely the combined presence of an elderly Italian population and a young, foreign population in precarious employment conditions that makes social cohesion such a difficult challenge and increases the perception of insecurity.

The second aspect is the spatial distribution of the difficult conditions and, consequently, of the inequalities they entail. Over time, many peripheral areas have been incorporated into the city and undergo either significant regeneration or, conversely, deterioration and downgrading. Neighbourhoods considered in the collective imagination as examples of peripheral conditions and social vulnerability have, over the years, been transformed into urban environments where the quality of life and degree of social cohesion are more than satisfactory. On the other hand, there are neighbourhoods—but also parts of neighbourhoods—where a combination of interconnected causes has led to a deterioration that is also a loss in aspirations by citizens (Appadurai 2004). What's more, the places that have suffered the most severe decline are now often close to the city centre, concentrated in territorial enclaves (a building, a few streets, sections of the historical centre, an area near the railway station, etc.) which are often difficult to identify in statistical terms and, in any case, not attributable to the traditional geography of neighbourhoods.

5.4 Peripheries in Milan

Unfortunately, it is not possible to provide empirical materials here to offer evidence of this reading of the disparities that have grown in the spatial and social forms of peripheral areas over recent years. However, an observation of the case of Milan confirms the elements that we have just identified (Pasqui 2018).

For Milan, peripheral conditions are not simply defined geographically (i.e. distance from the centre), nor do they coincide solely with social housing districts. In fact, some of the large public neighbourhoods are now liveable places, with high standards in terms of green spaces, services and good urban quality. Even neigh-bourhoods that have traditionally suffered from intense stigmatisation now boast far better conditions than they once did, largely thanks to efficient public policies and the committed work of determined, experienced actors. One such case is Ponte Lambro, a district in the south-east of the city of Milan. There are also enclaves of depriva-tion within largely regenerated neighbourhoods (as in the case of Via Bolla, in the Gallaratese district), or small areas very close to the centre with concentrated condi-tions of social precarity and fragility (Via Gola, Viale Bligny). Nowadays, it is often privately owned buildings in Milan that are worst affected by conditions of material deterioration and social deprivation. Often these areas are not located in the regional capital: to give just two examples, the Crocetta neighbourhood of Cinisello Balsamo or the Satellite neighbourhood of Pioltello could both be considered situations that represent a severe challenge for public policies.

As such, the new geographies of Milan's peripheries are often concentrated in municipalities other than the capital itself, which implies that the dynamics of periph-eralisation, in Milan's case, are strongly linked with processes of reconcentration. In order to understand this phenomenon, one must bear in mind that Milan is many different things at once, and that all of these can potentially contain processes which foster social and spatial inequalities.

Milan is first and foremost the central city, the regional capital which covers a small area (just 181 km^2, as opposed to Rome's 1285 km^2), still confined within its historical administrative boundaries consolidated over the first half of the twentieth century. A very strong narrative has developed around this city in recent years, deeply rooted in its long-established tradition and history, but also fuelled by a shift in expectations also perceived by international investors. For some observers, this Milan before pandemic was enjoying a "magical" age, ushered in by the iconic event of Expo 2015: a dynamic, welcoming city with a wealth of universities (just under 200,000 students are enrolled in Milan's nine universities, in addition to nearly 40,000 teaching and technical/administrative staff combined) and a variety of job opportunities (finance, fashion and design, the economies of culture and communication, health and all its related technologies). A city with a strong European identity that attracts not only foreign students, but also the temporary users who flock to its many successful events, as well as migrants and, more recently, tourists (over ten million in the metropolitan city alone in 2019), especially from abroad.

Over the years, this "small" Milan has gradually changed through molecular processes and mechanisms involving the social mobilisation of families and busi-nesses, rather than as the result of a comprehensive overall plan for the city. However, this central heart of the urban region has seen the strong growth of significant national and international investment in recent years. For example, Qatar's sovereign investment fund has acquired the entire Porta Nuova project for a market value that observers estimate to be around two billion Euros, but even smaller operations such as the opening of the Apple Store in Piazza Libertà, just a stone's throw from the Duomo, pay testament to how Milan has been launched back onto the radar of both major international financial investors and globalised multinationals.

It is here that social innovation processes find fertile ground, not least because of the permeability of its urban spaces. Nevertheless, even in this part of the city there are disused spaces, places that have fallen into deterioration and decline, even though the urban heart of Milan truly seems to be the focus of a small-scale renaissance, partly fostered by the redevelopment of spaces that had long been abandoned.

Of course, Milan is not this and this alone. Milan is also the city that extends, with its variable geometry, between the boundaries of the city proper and the conurbation of the municipalities in its first and second belts. It is in this city that some of the most important transformations have occurred or could yet occur, and it is here that the contrast between social and economic dynamism and new forms of inequality and fragility is at its starkest.

This intermediate city is the site of some major property development operations, that have not been suspended during COVID emergency: the residential developments in Cascina Merlata; the MIND project in the post-Expo area, headed up by Australian developer Landlease; the investments by large-scale retail chains in Arese and Cinisello Balsamo; the planned relocation of certain major hospitals to vacant areas between the city of Milan and the municipalities in the first belt, or to the Falck areas of Sesto San Giovanni. The metropolitan area is also home to peripheries old and new, characterised by social and economic fragility and cultures of resentment.

Milan is also a vast urban region that some important studies (Balducci et al. 2017) have defined as "post-metropolitan". It is an integrated urbanised area at the heart of Lombardy's manufacturing platform, where the balances and complementarities between the capital and the region have, over time, provided it with an extraordinary competitive edge. This Milan extends between the foothills (Novara, Varese, Como, Bergamo) and the irrigated plains (Pavia, Lodi, Piacenza), and is structured around an intricate environment of interrelationships, long and short networks, economic relationships between supply chains, and territorial clusters. It is precisely by observing these networks over the past few years that it has been possible to discern a risk of divergence between the city and the region, between Milan and its hinterland.

This large region is, in turn, part of an extended urban environment (a megacity, as Peter Hall would call it), stretching (at least) from Turin to Venice, in a logic of complementarity and competition in which functional connections play an essential role. In this region, the peripheries are often rural areas, small and medium-sized towns that are excluded from the metropolitan dynamics.

Finally, Milan is the gateway to global flows—a connector city located within international networks that go beyond geographical proximity and mobilise significant financial investments, but also flows of highly qualified human capital.

From the perspective of a post-pandemic scenario, each of these different ideas of Milan shows growing signs of polarisation and socio-spatial differentiation. In particular, COVID on the one hand risks exacerbating the crisis in relations between the capital city and its territory, whilst on the other, it brings the problems of segregation and socio-spatial fragility of the various peripheries to the fore.

5.5 Policy Suggestions

In this context of progressive fragilization of the peripheral areas, due in part to the pandemic forcibly accelerating processes that were already underway, it becomes important not only to recognise the central issues of the territorial dynamics of inequality in the peripheries following the pandemic, but also to propose strategies capable of assisting the peripheral areas most seriously affected by the pandemic with an approach that can use the resources set to be distributed over the coming years with an integrated, territorialised approach (Coppola et al. 2021).

Which path should we take if we wish to engage with the various dimensions of inequality in the urban peripheries after the pandemic and if we intend to develop effective public policies to tackle these problems? The Inequality and Diversity Forum report proposes relaunching a territorial approach for peripheral and inner areas (Barca 2009), "starting from the needs and aspirations of the people in these places". Implementing such an approach by suspending sectoral policies and piecing them back together into territorial development projects would mean "designing and implementing [...] development strategies in the peripheries that combine the improvement of fundamental services with the creation of opportunities for the fair and sustainable use of new technologies, with the local inhabitants strongly involved" (Inequality and Diversity Forum 2019: p. 97).

The perspective taken by the Forum is shared by many and assumes that the classic redistributive response is not sufficient to address territorial inequalities (Franzini et al. 2016). We need to carefully rethink and examine the phase of place-based urban policies that is now behind us in order to effectively recalibrate our interventions in this most critical current phase of urban policies, both national and European (Urban@it 2017, 2018, 2020).

To support an urban policy that reconciles innovation with inclusivity as much as possible, it is essential to implement public action focused on the regeneration of urban peripheries.

Indeed, urban regeneration programmes and projects for the most deeply affected peripheral areas in urban environments are not solely a matter of social policy. For one thing, they allow for the mobilisation of resources (first and foremost human capital) and the creation of new (and good) job opportunities. What's more, they reduce the risks associated with the costs (both economic and social) of inequality (Roberts et al. 2017).

Unlike what has happened in recent years with certain national programmes for peripheries in the last ten years ("Piano Città" i.e. City Plan; "Piano Periferie", i.e. Peripheries Plan), this should not be a case of finding emergency responses. Quite the contrary: it is necessary to build—patiently and working closely with local and regional authorities—integrated urban regeneration programmes for peripheral areas developed through participatory and place-based approaches.

In the final chapter, I will explore the issue of managing the vast amounts of EU resources over the coming years in greater depth. For now, I shall merely point out that over the next few years, tens of billions of Euros will descend upon urban areas, and the use of this money will have to be planned implementing projects that are not only fit for purpose, but also an effective way to spend the money.

An effective policy for reducing urban inequalities must engage the issue on three fronts with three drivers for change: employment, housing and schools.

The first driver is the construction of active employment and training policies on a suitable territorial scale, capable of intercepting as a priority the most fragile segments of peripheral populations, namely those excluded from the labour market or whose employment conditions are extremely precarious. Many experiments have been carried out on this front, but they have largely proven ineffective thus far because they often fail to accurately target the truly disadvantaged sections of the population. Place-based projects capable of generating good employment prospects in the peripheral areas of our cities should acknowledge that their central objective is the maintenance of facilities and material wellbeing (public buildings, sports facilities, parks and gardens, etc.). These could prove to be an important public investment in which the direct participation of the inhabitants in the improvement and upkeep of the places where they live and spend their time also becomes an opportunity to create more qualified, less precarious work (including through appropriate training courses).

The second driver is investment in housing. Housing-related deprivation and poverty are perhaps the most challenging obstacle to overcome for those living in the peripheries today. Although housing policies on a national scale are also crucial, regeneration projects and programmes financed by the Recovery Fund should also be able to promote impactful action at the local level.

Indeed, there is also a strongly rooted dimension to housing policies, in that they would require certain innovations in terms of management and administration capable of improving the living conditions of the worst-off and of creating significant experiences of mobilising underused local resources in an effort to improve the everyday lives of individuals and families.

Finally, the third driver is the patient, in-depth work on schools as powerful places of integration. Schools in peripheral areas are remarkable sounding boards for social innovation, where the mobilisation of volunteer work and social commitment find a privileged environment. This characteristic of schools should not, however, be considered in a vacuum: they are also places of conflict, where many compete for the scarce resources available. Acknowledging the conflicts and tensions in action means suppressing any nostalgia for community relations and closeness that cannot be reproduced in the context of the pluralisation of ways of living.

Despite this, it cannot be denied that schools are potential grounds for fertile inter-action between different people, where all can strive to achieve the delicate balance between universalistic needs and the proliferation of variety. As such, working in and on schools in peripheral areas means understanding not only how processes of socio-spatial segregation are affecting school systems in new ways, but also how schools can be interpreted as effective experimental platforms for welfare projects. In order to move in these different yet interconnected directions, investments and policies for schools—and in particular, for our school building stock—must adopt the character-istics of integrated regeneration and development projects. Projects of this kind would have the merit of activating administrative action in a concerted, coordinated way and would take on the role of integrated territorial interventions within the wider context of cohesion policies. By analogy with these policies, "school contracts" similar to "Neighbourhood contracts" (Contratti di quartiere) could be developed, following the example of what has already been done in some European cities. In this direction the experience of Contract Écoles in Brussels can be considered a benchmarking case. These policies could also be implemented in the form of competitive tenders, on the condition that schools suffering from situations of material deprivation and poor maintenance and those located in particularly poor urban environments are given priority access to funding.

References

Appadurai A (2004) The capacity to aspire: culture and the terms of recognition. In: Rao Y, Walton M (eds) Culture and public. Stanford University Press, Stanford CA, pp 59–84
Balducci A, Fedeli V, Curci F (eds) (2017) Post-metropolitan territories: looking for a new urbanity. Routledge, London
Barca F (2009) An agenda for the reform of cohesion policy. A place-based approach to meeting European union challenges and expectations. European Commission, Independent Report, Bruxelles
Camera dei Deputati (2018) Relazione della Commissione parlamentare di inchiesta sulle condizioni di sicurezza e sullo stato di degrado delle città e delle loro periferie. Roma
Coppola A, Del Fabbro M, Lanzani A, Pessina G, Zanfi F (a cura di) (2021) Ricomporre i divari. Politiche e progetti territoriali contro le disuguaglianze e per la transizione ecologica. Il Mulino, Bologna
Department for Cohesion Policies _ Dipartimento per le Politiche di Coesione (2017) Poverty maps. Analisi territoriale del disagio socio-economico delle aree urbane. Roma
European Commission (2017) My region, My Europe, our future: the seventh report on economic, social and territorial cohesion. Brussels
Inequality and Diversity Forum (2019) 15 proposte per la giustizia sociale. Roma
Franzini M, Granaglia E, Raitano M (2016) Extreme inequalities in contemporary capitalism. Springer, Berlin
Iammarino S, Rodríguez-Pose A, Storper M (2017), Why regional development matters for Europe's economic future. European Commission, Working Papers, WP 07/2017, Bruxelles
ISTAT (2017), Materiali per la Commissione parlamentare di inchiesta sulle condizioni di sicurezza e sullo stato di degrado delle città e delle loro periferie, Roma
Pasqui G (2018) Raccontare Milano. Progetti, politiche, immaginari. Franco Angeli, Milano
Petrillo A (2018) La periferia nuova. Disuguaglianza, spazi, città. Franco Angeli, Milano
Petrillo A (2020) La periferia non è più quella di un tempo. Bordeaux, Roma
Piketty T (2015) The Economics of Inequality. Harvard University Press, Cambridge (US)
Roberts P, Sykes H, Granger R. (eds) (2017) Urban Regeneration. A Handbook. Sage, London
Rodríguez-Pose A (2017) The revenge of the place that don't matter (and what to do about it). Camb J Reg Econ Soc 11(1):189–209
Secchi B (2005) La città del XX secolo. Laterza, Bari
Urban@it (2017) II Rapporto sulle città italiane. Le agende urbane delle città italiane. Il Mulino, Bologna
Urban@it (2018), III Rapporto sulle città italiane. Mind the gap. Il distacco tra politiche e città. Il Mulino, Bologna
Urban@it (2020) V Rapporto sulle città italiane. Politiche urbane per le periferie. Il Mulino, Bologna

Chapter 6
Planning: Preparedness

Abstract The chapter offers some critical considerations regarding the effects of pandemic on planning cultures and practices. The concept of preparedness, introduced in the recent international debate, is used as a tool for strengthening forms of planning that take the objective of preparing societies and territories in a context of radical uncertainty and instability. The concept of preparedness is also used for reflecting on the public action dilemmas connected with the introduction, during the pandemic crisis, of actions based on a "state of exception" logic. In the last part of the chapter are proposed some principles for spatial planning coping with COVID-19 challenges.

6.1 Planning and the Pandemic: The Role of the Public Sector

During the first lockdown, in the initial months of the devastation of 2020, during the phase in which fear and despair, but also the pressing need not to feel powerless, sparked some ingenious and often visionary reflections on what was going on (Harvey 2020; Latour 2020; Morin 2020; Florida et al. 2021), an issue that had long been silenced and removed from political and cultural debate very much returned to the fore: in the face of global crises which affect the lives of entire communities and result in pervasive, long-term effects, we need the help of the state and its institutions, in all their articulated territorial forms. The pandemic has led to an overwhelming demand for public action.

We need the public sector because, to put it in economic terms, the market is simply not capable—and has no intention of guaranteeing the provision of the kinds of public assets (starting with healthcare and minimum social welfare conditions for all) that are very expensive to produce and relatively unprofitable to offer.

COVID-19 is tangible evidence of the failure of a model of global capitalism that is incapable of insuring and reinsuring itself against risk (not only as regards pandemics, but also in relation to the unpredictable effects of climate change). The events of the past year have once again shifted the focus squarely onto the issue of the public sector, of the role and significance of public action in the regulation, governance and design of our societies, and in particular, as far as I am concerned, the city, the territory and the landscape.

Of course, not all the actors involved—and crucially, not all countries—shared this perspective, at least not in the first few months of the pandemic. Some primarily the United States, which is now more than ever in the thick of a crisis of meaning and perspectives (Cartosio 2020)—even adopted a denialistic perspective at the start, though this has largely been overcome, including at the ballot box with the election of Joe Biden.

However, there is no denying that the dominion, the sad fact of the rich and powerful prevailing in the war against the poor (D'Eramo 2020), has, over the last few decades, resulted in public action being deprived of not only its resources, but also its cultures, amongst which a thought that fits in perfectly with the questions that we now endlessly turn over in our heads: what can we plan? How can we plan?

Of course, the disappearance of a culture of planning should not prevent us from also seeing the trials and errors that the theories and practices of territorial and socio-economic planning have put in place over the last few decades, including in Italy. Consider, for example, the so-called "new planning" approach inaugurated by Carlo Azeglio Ciampi in the mid-1990s, which—albeit with many limits attempted to restore the significant role that public investment once played in supporting territorial development processes (Palermo and Ponzini 2010). Recognising the merits and limitations of that perspective (Barca 2009), which is largely behind us now, undoubtedly represents a good stepping stone as we seek to understand how to once again pick up the thread of a new wave of public action which will—at least in Europe—be able to benefit from investments and resources of sizeable proportions.

How, then, can we consider the possibilities and limitations of our planning action, here and now? How can we restore the centrality of public action in this time of crisis so similar to, and yet so different from, the previous global crisis from the end of the first decade of this century, which so profoundly redefined the features and mechanisms of our economic and social formation focused on financially-driven globalised capitalism?

I have already mentioned in previous chapters that the first step to be taken is to cast aside the idea that all of society's problems can be resolved without, or even against, the public sector. The financial, organizational and cognitive weakening of public actors has greatly undermined the effectiveness as well as the efficiency of public action.

Abandoning the idea that public intervention is a problem is not, however, a matter for the verbal sparring of a cultural debate. The stakes are unspeakably high: the balances of power on a worldwide scale, practices of control and domination that have intensified deep inequalities (Piketty 2015), power relations between social classes and crises of agency for any and all radically alternative perspectives, both in individual nation states and on a global scale. We must never lose sight of all this, lest the discussion on the return of the public sector become abstract and academic.

Shrugging off the lexicon and the atmosphere that have dominated public discourse at this crucial moment, as capitalist globalisation is poised to reach its peak, is, however, only one of the necessary conditions. In my opinion, it is also a matter of thinking about our circumstances within a wider timeframe, considering a whole host of variables—first and foremost demographic and technological ones—which have profoundly altered the relationship between mankind, nature and artefacts on a global scale.

This backdrop to the discussion is, in my view, inescapable, if we want to truly understand the nature of that radical upheaval in forms of living that Bruno Latour recently explored by mobilising the concept of the "terrestrial" (Latour 2017) and that Ash Amin and Nigel Thrift used to propose the idea of observing the world's urbanisation processes "through the eyes of the city" (Amin and Thrift 2016).

The context offered by Serres, the backdrop of the anthropological transformation that I presented in Chap. 2, must be considered in combination with the dynamics of power and the war waged by the rich upon the poor which I mentioned earlier, and which Serres certainly tends to underestimate.

This anthropological, technological and demographic transformation, which Serres sometimes refers to as "hominescence" (Serres 2001), is intimately intertwined with our inability to insure ourselves against risk under conditions of radical uncertainty (or even ontological uncertainty, as analytical philosophers would call it: Chiffi and Chiodo 2020).

Technological change, the environmental crisis, pandemics, in their inextricable interaction between the natural and social dimensions, challenge our ability to predict the future, and thus also our capacity to plan our actions and responses. All the data that we now know how to store, handle and manipulate as never before is still not enough to deal with the event—this pandemic, for example, and all its unpredictable consequences. The event, which I already touched upon in Chap. 2, is precisely that which happens without us expecting it—that which slips into our lives in the night, like an unexpected guest. It is the invasion of the Other, surprising us, redefining us. Jacques Derrida's entire reflection on hospitality, on the event as the occurrence of the wholly "other", should be reinterpreted as an ontology of the impossible (Derrida and Dufourmantelle 2000).

One might counter by saying that we have known for a very long time that we cannot truly plan the future—that uncertainty, due for example to the complexity and numerousness of the information and relationships that we have to take into consideration, to the limits of our knowledge and our ability for calculation, does not allow us to plan in any sort of effective way.

Without needing to resort to von Hayek (1948), and without forgetting how much his positions fueled the conservative revolution, the reflection on the unexpected effects of social action (Boudon 1984) and the Anglo-Saxon debate on urban planning itself from Melvin Webber (Rittel and Webber 1973) to the radical positions of the late 1960s (Crosta 1973) onwards have shed light on the technical and political limits of comprehensive planning, partly due to its technocratic nature and its faith in the power of technology and calculation, but also due to its intrinsically ideological dimension.

On the other hand, the three great "irregulars" of the Anglo-Saxon social sciences of the twentieth century had already buried comprehensive planning under the "hiding hand" (Hirschman 1967), in the folds of "muddling through" (Lindblom 1959), and on the wave of the need to "deschool" society and expose the false idols of scientists, engineers and planners (Illich 1971).

The long goodbye to comprehensive planning should be a widely accepted fact by now. And yet, here and now, we need to go back and reflect on that debate, and in order to do so, we need to think about how to prepare ourselves for the event.

6.2 Rethinking Preparedness

What does it mean to be prepared? Alessandro Balducci, in some of his recent reflections, invited us to make use of the concept of preparedness (Lakoff 2007, 2017), in the framework of a meditation on planning post-COVID and, more generally, with a view to resilience (Balducci 2020).

> The current pandemic, together with the other 'unprecedented' situations we have experienced all over the world, from the devastating fires of Australia and the U.S. in recent months, to the 2010 tsunami and nuclear accident in Japan, to terrorist attacks in France in 2015, demonstrate that if conventional forms of planning are not effective, and we cannot even draw much from the indications of strategic planning, we still need to be prepared; we still need to develop a capacity to react to the unexpected (Balducci 2020: 23).

Using a concept that originally emerged in the field of healthcare, Balducci emphasises that talking about preparedness means thinking about an approach to the imponderability of the crises that may arise that aims not to avoid them—which would be impossible—but rather to build up a capacity for reaction that is valid in the most diverse range of post-catastrophe situations.

> A form of planning that takes on the objective of preparing for the unexpected through scenario construction, the protection of critical communication infrastructures, the provision of devices that facilitate coping in different types of emergency, commissioning immediately activated alarm systems, systems for coordinating different subject, and periodic verification of these operations. [...] Preparedness for the incalculable disasters arising amidst growing social, economic and environmental instability means constructing not the solution, bit the capacity to react in the face of the things we don't know we don't know (Balducci 2020: 24).

Following a line of reflection that also makes use of the results of interpretative theories of organisation forced to contend with changeable conditions and vague situations tackled the subject by introducing the concept of "negative capacity", specifically in reference to a case of post-catastrophic social mobilisation (Lanzara 1993), Balducci proposes a suggestion of rethinking the activity of planning so as to shift its aim towards preparing for the unexpected, working both on the construction of tools and on effective social interaction mechanisms.

Ash Amin, amongst others, offered a sensitive reflection on the potential ambiguities of the concept of preparedness, pointing out the conditions under which a culture of being prepared can also be used as a tool for democratisation.

In the paragraph entitled "From Protection to Preparedness" in *Land of Strangers*, Amin points out that securing both citizens and borders was an obsession shared by many Western governments throughout the second half of the twentieth century. Based on this context, too—in which the nuclear threat has gradually been joined by other types of natural and social risks—a widespread culture of risk management has grown enormously; in Amin's view, this has shifted the emphasis from the perspective of providing universalistic services to that of building tools to increase individual resilience in the face of adversity.

From this point of view, the move from the logic of insurance against risk to that of preparedness for it represents an interesting element of innovation, on account of the "transition from a culture of total protection and risk avoidance to one of joint responsibility and risk mitigation" (Amin 2012: 146).

If we consider preparedness to be a form of shared responsibility, we must nonetheless be mindful of how it can be used in an ideological and manipulative way. As Amin writes, we are invited to

> … [rethink] the meaning of preparedness for a turbulent future. Today, it has come to signify - at least in the neoliberal world - preparing for the worst and aggressively pushing back at identifiable sources of harm, while accepting that some sacrifices are sources (usually the vulnerable and undefended). This thinking needs to be reversed by adding more anticipatory and protective measures to the available arsenal, by minimising the potential of damage and maximising the capacity to resist and recover. If such thinking takes us back to arguments for central planning and state responsibility, extensive expertise, comprehensive insurance and protection, precautionary and peaceful actions, automated maintenance and repair, let it do so, without temptation to be apologetic, ashamed about some putative return to an age of centrism (Amin 2012: 162–163).

From this point of view, I feel that the perspective proposed by Balducci—revisited through the lens of Ash Amin's precautions—is of great interest because it assumes the need for institutions and society to be open to the possible, but also to the unpredictable, considering uncertainty not as an exceptional state, but as the permanent condition of our existence on earth (Veca 1997). An uncertainty that has to do with the consideration of the radical finiteness our species, our knowledge and our resources (Pievani 2020).

Making sense of action means engaging in a process of sensemaking which, as organisational scholar Karl E. Weick wrote, is always a posthumous and retrospective act (Weick 1995). In order to be prepared, we must therefore learn to give a reason to what we do, to work on the sense of what happens (to us) before and whilst we work on the technical solution to problems.

As such, a reflection on planning of any kind must clear the field of a misunderstanding: it is not simply a case of reverting to our reliance on (supposedly) expert knowledge and skills. It is a question of monitoring all the knowledge mobilised and produced, of unmasking the now-rife anti-scientific attitudes of an ideological and regressive nature, but also of carving out a space for public discussion that does not fall victim to the dictatorship of competencies and that recognises its own field of political decision-making and public responsibility.

6.3   Risks and Democracy

In the reflection on planning, and particularly on the practices employed in governing the territories, the need has long since become clear to govern for the short term and the long term together; to reconcile the facets of a strategic operation and a tactical one; to embrace uncertainty as the terrain on which to operate with an experimental and incremental approach.

Whilst these may be very general principles, they can nonetheless serve as guidelines for the construction of a renewed culture of planning in all its forms, but also to combat three risks.

The first risk is that of a return to the logic of comprehensive and scientific planning, which is often a cover for political and ideological motivations. Models, data and evidence can be easily manipulated, used mindlessly without consideration of their true significance. What's more, in the past we have already experienced the failure of rationality imposed from above: all the more reason why it seems to be inadequate in a context of radical uncertainty. So it is by no means a question of returning to comprehensive planning: we should have learnt by now that there is never a linear sequence between knowledge, decision and action (Crosta 1995). Recursively, knowledge (specifically different forms thereof), decisions and actions all play out within complex systems of action involving multiple actors.

The second risk—apparently contrary to but in actual fact complementary to the first—is that of haste, of the demand for quick decisions, of special dispensations, of exceptional decision-making processes. Without prejudice to the need to reduce the cumbersome weight and flaws of bureaucracy, insisting on planning in a "state of exception" so as to simplify processes has often proven illusory, as demonstrated by the many instances of receivership that have punctuated the affairs of my country. Perhaps more crucially, carrying out these sorts of planning activities in a state of exception only bolsters the influence of lobbies and powerful groups, especially in a context in which, for the first time in decades, we will have significant public resources at our disposal. However, I feel that it is essential to keep a close eye on whether and how a delicate balance is maintained, namely that between the decisions made within the rhetorical context of the general interest and the need to safeguard the principles and mechanisms of polyarchal democracy from the logic of permanent exception. Without following Giorgio Agamben (2020) and other critical voices that have identified the public sanitary intervention with an authoritarian strategy of control, we can always heed the warnings of a liberal such as Robert Dahl (1998), who suggest to suspect scientifically or technically driven public decisions.

The third risk, which I am especially keen to point out due to my specific interests, but which I believe is also essential in more general terms, is that of building planning tools that are blind to the complexities and variety of the different territories. We are faced with the disastrous prospect of seeing projects, plans and policies simplified with no regard for the territorial nature of the problems and solutions involved, much as we have in recent months. If this proves to be the case, I am quite certain that the effectiveness of public action and planning will be markedly reduced, all without increasing its efficiency in exchange.

6.4 Principles for Action

Based on the lessons that we should have learned, and in light of the risks that we are running, I propose a number of principles for action for consideration, each of which should prove useful for experimenting with a concrete and effective approach to the new phase of planning that we have before us:

- immediately starting to roll out experimental, reversible actions that can test out a variety of tools and solutions. From this perspective, to give an example, infrastructuring does not mean deferring to the logic of large-scale works, which risks being ineffective, but rather investing in the reinfrastructuring and exceptional maintenance of our cities and territories, with an approach rooted in principles of ecological transition;
- always bearing in mind the real-world effects on everyday life of any actions, projects and initiatives, from a perspective that is attentive to the materiality of the relationship between forms of space and ordinary practices. This means having an accurate understanding of how aspects such as the organisation of work, mobility, schools, and the use of parks and open spaces actually work. This close-to-practice, experiential approach must incorporate analytical evidence, data and models with a view to building solutions deemed plausible and credible for those who have to implement and interact with them in everyday life;
- building territorial projects in which the actions and solutions implemented are specifically suited to the variety of resources and problems at hand. This implies a capacity for interinstitutional cooperation, but also specific skills (in terms of content and process, as well as procedure) which are often lacking in public administration today and which the resources available could be used to consolidate;
- working on our territories' ability to prepare themselves by designing territorial networks not only in terms of social and healthcare, but also with regard to mobility, forms of work and services. In order to do this, it is also essential to work with people and families, helping to empower them with regard to the conditions of the ongoing emergency and the effects of the economic crisis that is already affecting the lives and futures of the most vulnerable in society;
- engaging the involvement of the social forces, intermediate bodies, and networks of associations and volunteers that have mobilised in recent months as a resource rather than an obstacle, because the complexity of the processes at work is an extraordinary resource for collective learning, legitimisation and effectiveness when it comes to their implementation.

In short, an incremental, possibilistic, experimental, open and contextual idea of planning that is closely intertwined with concrete forms of living and capable of embracing the pluralistic nature of our interests and volitions. But also one that is guided by politics rather than technology, because it is only under these conditions that it can be able to work here and now, in these specific conditions, but also to produce visions of a different future.

These principles need to be concretely tested out in complex, multi-actor processes which take the territorial dimension as their determining factor. Expert knowledge, including academic one, can and must be put at the service of this approach to planning in all its forms.

Needless to say, it will be no mean feat: what is at stake is not a reform of territorial welfare, but the potentially catastrophic end of a model of development that is on the cusp of becoming obsolete. It is only by identifying and embracing the interconnections between economies, societies and territories that we will be put in a position to open the door to a way of thinking and acting that is suited to these difficult times.

References

Agamben G (2020) A che punto siamo? L'epidemia come politica. Quodlibet, Macerata

Amin A (2012) Land of Strangers. Polity Press, London

Amin A, Thrift N (2016) Seeing like a City. Polity Press, London

Balducci A (2020) Planning for resilience. In Balducci A, Chiffi D, Curci F (eds.) Risk and resilience, Springer Brief, Berlin-Milano, pp 15–25

Barca F (2009) An Agenda for the reform of cohesion policy. A place-based approach to meeting European Union challenges and expectations. European Commission, Independent Report, Bruxelles

Boudon P (1984) La place du desordre. PUF, Paris

Cartosio B (2020) Dollari e no. Gli Stati Uniti dopo la fine del secolo americano. DeriveApprodi, Roma

Chiffi D, Chiodo S (2020), Risk and uncertainty. Foundational issues. In Balducci A, Chiffi D, Curci F (eds) Risk and resilience. Springer Brief, Berlin-Milano, p 1–13

Crosta PL (ed) (1973), L'urbanista di parte. Ruolo sociale del tecnico e partecipazione popolare nei processi di pianificazione urbana. Franco Angeli, Milano

Crosta PL (1995) La politica del piano. Franco Angeli, Milano

Dahl R (1998) On democracy. Yale University Press, Yale

D'Eramo M (2020) Dominio. La guerra invisibile dei potenti contro i sudditi. Feltrinelli, Milano

Derrida J, Dufourmantelle A (2000) On ospitality. Stanford Univ. Press, Stanford

Florida R, Rodríguez-Pose A, Storper M (2021) Cities in a post-Covid world. Urban Studies. Forthcoming

Harvey D (2020) Anti-capitalistic politics in the time of Covid-19. Jacobin https://jacobinmag.com/2020/03/david-harvey-coronavirus-political-economy-disruptions. Accessed 31 July 2021

Hayek von F (1948) Individualism and Economic Order. University of Chicago Press, Chicago

Hirschman A (1967) Development projects observed. The Brookings Institute, Washington

Illich I (1971) Deschooling society. Penguin, London

Lakoff A (2007) Preparing for the next emergency. Publ Cult 19(2):247–271

Lakoff A (2017) Unprepared: global health in a time of emergency. University of California Press, Berkley

Lanzara GF (1993) Capacità negativa. Competenza progettuale e modelli di intervento nelle organizzazioni. Il Mulino, Bologna

Latour B (2017) Où atterrir? Comment s'orienter in politique. Le Découverte, Paris

Latour B (2020) Immaginare gesti-barriera contro il ritorno alla produzione pre-crisi Antinomie. https://antinomie.it/index.php/2020/04/09/immaginare-gesti-barriera-contro-il-ritorno-alla-pro duzione-pre-crisi/. Accessed 9 Apr 2020

Lindblom C (1959) The science of 'muddling through.' Public Administrative Review 19(2):79–88

Morin E (2020) Changeons de voie: les leçons du coronavirus. Denoiel, Paris

Palermo PC, Ponzini D (2010) Spatial planning and urban development. Springer, Berlin

Pievani T (2020) Finitudine. Un romanzo filosofico su fragilità e libertà. Cortina Editore, Milano

Piketty T (2015) The economics of inequality. Harvard University Press, Cambridge (US)

Rittel HW, Webber M (1973) Dilemmas in a general theory of planning. Policy Sci 4(2):155–169

Serres M (2001) Hominescence. La Pommier, Paris

Veca S (1997) Dell'incertezza. Tre meditazioni filosofiche. Feltrinelli, Milano

Weick KE (1995) Sensemaking in organisations. Sage Publications Thousand Oaks (CA)

Chapter 7
Policies: Antifragility

Abstract Starting from the research activities undertaken in the framework of the Department of Excellence—"Territorial fragility" project, the chapter discusses the concept of "anti-fragility" as a tool for planning practices accepting radical uncertainty and capable of engaging with unexpected events and disorder. The anti-fragile approach is used to reflect of planning strategies able to use effectively the huge financial resources that UE programs (Next Generation EU and 2021–2027 Structural Funds) will make available to our cities in the next years.

7.1 (Territorial) Fragility

The effects produced by the pandemic differ according to the degree of fragility of the cities and territories. The more a given region, city or neighbourhood showed signs of fragility, the more this catastrophic event generated—and continues to generate negative impacts on its people and places. Evaluating the connection between fragility and the pandemic in the urban dimension first of all requires a solid grasp of the specific nature of these territories' fragilities, advocating for a culture of planning capable of tackling the challenges posed by these fragilities.

In the framework of the Departments of Excellence—"Territorial Fragilities" project run by the Department of Architecture and Urban Studies at Politecnico di Milano, the specificity of the notion of the fragilities of our cities and territories has been addressed in several forms. I would like to use this notion as a springboard for my reflections on antifragile plans, policies and projects for post-pandemic cities and territories.

First of all, the notion of fragility has more than one ambiguous feature, and as such needs to be qualified. An object or a person is fragile when it is susceptible to breaking, fracturing and splintering; for instance, the stem of a flower or the bone of an aging animal. Yet a vase, a building or a bridge may also be fragile, or even a landscape, a ridge, a valley or a neighbourhood. What is meant by the idea of fragility? How does it differ from the idea of vulnerable or risky? On this issue, recent contributions by Infussi (2019) as well as Chiffi and Curci (2019) help us to

G. Pasqui, *Coping with the Pandemic in Fragile Cities*, PoliMI SpringerBriefs, https://doi.org/10.1007/978-3-030-93979-3_7

isolate the peculiar nature of the notion of fragility, along with its connection with the topic of radical uncertainty explored in Chap. 1 of this volume.

First of all, as Chiffi and Curci write, "fragility proves to be a multidimensional concept; this is why we have various solutions at our disposal aimed at averting fragility, some based on preventative measures, others on genuine alternatives to it" (Chiffi and Curci 2019: 57). As such, acknowledging the close connection between fragility and uncertainty seems to invalidate the traditional notions of the logic of risk for our purposes. Indeed, as Curci and Chiffi observe:

> All in all, notions such as probability, expected utility, damage and consequence assessment can be very problematic when applied to the concept of fragility. This does not mean that probabilistic risk estimates are always useless for an analysis of fragility; however, they are clearly not the only tool available, nor do they represent the most appropriate method to follow. Fragility-related issues appear to be closer to fundamental uncertainty in nature and have some affinities with so-called 'wicked problems' (Chiffi and Curci 2019: 58).

In his text, Infussi starts by offering a definition of fragility as "the predisposition of an object or a situation to change its state and constitutive characteristics, even radically, as a result of unexpected accidental events" (Infussi 2019: 61). He also distinguishes three variations of fragility. In the first, fragility is a constitutive characteristic of the object or situation, an "original state" that is exposed to the risk posed by human action or by nature. A second form considers fragility to be related to a process in which an object or a context moves away from an original equilibrium due to conditions that disrupt this equilibrium. As a Spinozian ontology suggests (Deleuze 1990) if we consider bodies as unstable collections of constitutive relationships ever subjected to encounters that can consolidate or break these bonds, fragility as an emergent state is the result of "bad encounters" that can be endogenous or exogenous in nature. Finally, fragility may have to do with the interruption of a process of evolution and consolidation that is still very much under development, not yet having reached its stable or equilibrium state.

The effects of the pandemic on cities—understood as complex assemblages of objects, technologies, social relationships, institutions and regulatory systems—could be correlated with each of these three meanings of fragility. The cities exposed to the pandemic, especially in some parts, such as the peripheral areas that I discussed in Chap. 5, are characterised by a fragility in their very constitution. On the other hand, as demonstrated by the pandemic's effects on urban rhythms and practices of movement, in recent months cities have become more fragile, more exposed to processes of loss of cohesion compared with previous conditions, with significant effects on their activities, practices, and ways of relating.

Any observation of the current and future effects of the pandemic must also be in a position to understand the functioning of the processes at work from multiple points of view: structurally, of course, but also the perspective of everyday life, of the way in which we inhabit urban space together.

From this perspective, fragility is connected to life (the life of people, communities and territories), because fragilities concern processes and dynamics, and are not static in nature. For these reasons, the first task is to establish a general definition of (territorial) fragility that can cover all its various shapes and forms.

What does it mean, then, to observe the pandemic-stricken city from the point of view of *territorial* fragilities? Why is the connotation of territoriality important here? Firstly, because the fragility that we are exploring is an urban fragility, and cities can, in turn, be defined as collections of surfaces and practices, history and technologies, nature and culture. It is precisely because territories cannot be reduced to a single dimension (the hydrogeological aspect, the seismic aspect, the landscape aspect, the social aspect, the housing aspect, etc.) that they can exhibit so many forms of fragility, all interconnected.

Indeed, one of the goals of the "Territorial Fragilities" programme is to better clarify the interrelationship between different dimensions of fragility, but also to explore how a truly transdisciplinary research project—taking its cues from the problems and issues involved rather than the disciplines, with all their limitations and specialisations—can contribute to better defining characteristics, dynamics and prospects for action.

As such, one of the crucial aspects is to outline different geographies of fragility: that is, different ways of describing the Italian and European territory that are even capable of subverting their traditional representations.

Secondly, the fragility of territories is characterised not only by different spatialities, but also by multiple temporalities. A given territory can remain fragile for a long time, for decades or even centuries. Meanwhile, in another, fragility can lead to a very sudden and radical change of state.

In certain ways, a territory's fragility dictates its tempo, defining its possibilities and bifurcations, outlining its states of disequilibrium, its catastrophic conditions (where the sense of catastrophes is that of mathematical theory: Thom 1989).

One of the tasks we should be undertaking is to understand the processual nature of fragility, which is at once a condition (a state of ongoing potential disequilibrium), a result (of processes, but also of policies), and a possibility (in relation to a situation of radical uncertainty).

From this point of view, one of the results of this work of analysis and planning should be to tell stories of fragility by means of some sort of biographies of fragile territories. History matters!

Moreover, with respect to the territorial connotation of fragility, it is important to recognise that there are many dimensions of fragility. Arturo Lanzani, in the "Territorial Fragilities" section of the book *Manifesto per riabitare l'Italia* [*Manifesto for Reinhabiting Italy*] (Cersosimo and Donzelli 2020; Lanzani 2020), identifies five dimensions: demographic, socio-economic, environmental, mobility-related, and socio-settlement and landscape-related.

Faced once again with this plural nature of fragility, there are multiple operations to be undertaken: recognising the possible reciprocal and circular causalities between these dimensions, specific to the individual territorial contexts; identifying and describing the multiple geographies that outline different ways of articulating the various dimensions; understanding how to act with an integrated approach to the various dimensions.

Finally, it is a matter of understanding how considering the situation through the lens of the link between fragility and the effects of the pandemic challenges our seven forms of rationality, as touched upon in previous chapters (Balducci et al. 2020).

7.2 Antifragile

Nassim Nicholas Taleb's books *The Black Swan: The Impact of the Highly Improbable* (2012b) and *Antifragile: Things That Gain from Disorder* (2012a) have seen considerable success, including in the field of planning theory. As many people know, Taleb undertakes to distinguish fragility from robustness and antifragility, starting from the assumption that everything (individual objects, living organisms, natural and manmade systems) is subject to unpredictable events whose existence constitutes a condition of disorder.

The pandemic can, of course, be considered one of these disorder-generating events, although I am not wholly convinced that it can be called a "black swan". Looking at the international news since September 2001, we can safely say that there has been an incredible number of black swans. A report entitled "The Human Cost of Disasters 2000–2019", published by the United Nations Office for Disaster Risk Reduction (UNDDR) and the Centre for Research on the Epidemiology of Disasters (CRED) to mark the International Day for Disaster Risk Reduction, confirms that meteorological events are now the predominant type of disaster in the twenty-first century (UNDDR 2020) and highlights how the number of natural catastrophic events—many of which are climate-related—has multiplied over the last twenty years. Extreme weather phenomena and natural disasters have increased dramatically over the last twenty years. Moreover, the trend continues, fully confirming the predictions consistently made by scientists. For years, they have been explaining that one of the consequences of global warming would be an increase in both the frequency and the intensity of droughts, hurricanes, floods and the like. All in all, 7348 large-scale disasters—resulting in a combined 1.23 million deaths—were included in the review. But the total number of people affected in a range of other ways proved significantly higher, at over four billion worldwide. And the damage caused by these extreme events is colossal: $2.97 billion in economic losses alone.

The years 2004, 2008 and 2010 were the worst, having had over 200,000 deaths each as a result of natural disasters. The largest single event in terms of the number of victims was the Indian Ocean tsunami of 2004, with 226,400 deaths; the second was the magnitude-7.0 earthquake that struck an already poverty-stricken Haiti in the middle of the night in 2010, causing some 222,000 deaths and making millions homeless. In 2008, Cyclone Nargis in Myanmar killed more than 138,000 people. From 2000 to 2019, the average number of deaths from natural disasters worldwide was around 60,000 per year, although there have been no mega disasters causing at least 100,000 deaths since 2010, and in no year since then has the figure ever exceeded 35,000 deaths.

But natural disasters are far from the only threat. The great global financial and then economic crisis, which shook economies and financial markets the world over from 2007 onwards, can also in many ways be considered an extreme event, and one which has further exacerbating the inequalities between regions.

Extreme phenomena—be they social or natural—that are characterised by a high degree of uncertainty and unpredictability test our predictive abilities and our propensity to insure ourselves against risk in the harshest of ways.

From this point of view, the pandemic has provided us with an opportunity to think more radically about the need to overhaul our very idea of planning. According to Taleb, an object, an organism, or a natural or manmade artificial system can be said to be fragile if events, disturbances, stress factors and disorder can essentially be harmful to it. However, there are two concepts that could be considered the opposite of fragility. The first family of concepts revolves around the notion of "robustness". Robust, durable, resistant, even resilient to some extent, are properties that allude to the subject's imperviousness to the event, which may not harm it, but will not bring it any benefit either.

"Antifragile", unlike "robust", can be used to describe anything which, under certain circumstances and conditions, can actually flourish in disorder, improving its performance precisely because of its interaction with unpredictable events and under conditions of radical uncertainty.

> Some things benefit from shocks; they thrive and grow when exposed to volatility, random-ness, disorder, and stressors and love adventure, risk and uncertainty. Yet, in spite of the ubiquity of the phenomenon, there is no word for the exact opposite of fragile. Let us call it anti-fragile. Anti-fragility is beyond resilience or robustness. The resilient resists shocks and stays the same; the anti-fragile gets better (Taleb 2012, 3).

How can we best exploit the concept of antifragility in the field of planning? And why might it be useful to us? First of all, the pandemic—as highlighted in other chapters of this book—brought about a significant paradigm shift, at least within Europe, with regard to public investment and intervention, providing member states with a quantity of resources that had never been made available in the thirty years prior.

It is therefore a matter of using these resources effectively, and doing so requires planning for the future. However, we must first understand what kind of planning we most need, given that it is a question of coming up with plans and schemes for complex social and territorial systems in the absence of a strong ability to predict the future. As Ivan Blečić and Arnaldo Cecchini write in a volume that programmatically sets out to imagine how an antifragile approach to planning would look (Blečić and Cecchini 2016), we must think about the future without foreseeing it, making use of the now extremely long-standing debate on the limits of rational planning and embracing the need to accept a weak capacity for prediction as a guideline for action.

Blečić and Cecchini believe that antifragile planning accepts radical uncertainty as an unavoidable fact, and they propose three main moves for experimenting with forms of planning that are capable of tackling—or rather, engaging with—disorder.

First of all, antifragile planning advocates for a negative way, i.e. the ability to offer indications about what it would be best to avoid doing through rules and restrictions capable of fostering resilience and antifragility, limiting superfluous rules as much as possible and establishing a framework of long-term rules and standards—all precautionary in nature—that are also able to incorporate some principles of fairness and equality.

Secondly, antifragile planning adopts a principle for action consisting of establishing a set of desired scenarios—shared visions which it is hoped will come to fruition. These shared urban visions are aimed at increasing empowerment, according to Amartya Sen's view, by involving the inhabitants as agents of the transformational process.

Finally, when faced with negative rules and the production of visions, it is planning that provides the flexibility needed not only to allow social actors their autonomy, but also to permit social and institutional actors to generate and implement good ideas. Planning is therefore the ground for concrete experimentation with different plans for living.

This is not the place for an analytical discussion of Blečić and Cecchini's perspective. However, it does help us to understand how we can accept the necessity and inescapable nature of planning from a perspective that has left behind any and all pretensions of being comprehensive, as well as the hypothesis of institutions managing society in an effective way.

7.3 European Investments and Planning: A Tricky Challenge

The theoretical considerations laid out above paint a picture in which it is crucial for planning cultures to be reconsidered and overhauled. This is happening in a context in which, for the first time since the years immediately following the end of World War II, Europe will be able to use a massive amount of public investment to tackle the effects of the pandemic.

Next Generation EU is the European Commission's plan to escape from the wake of the pandemic, involving a seven-year commitment totalling €806.9 billion. On 13 July 2021, 12 EU countries—Austria, Belgium, Denmark, France, Germany, Greece, Italy, Latvia, Luxembourg, Portugal, Slovakia and Spain—were given the green light to use the EU recovery and resilience funds to kickstart their economies and recover from the consequences of COVID-19. Thanks to the adoption of Implementing Decisions made by the Council on the approval of plans, member states can enter into grant agreements and loan agreements that will allow for up to 13% of the total amount to be pre-funded. These figures—unthinkable up to just a few years ago—will allow Italy to have access to a share equivalent to approximately 28% of the total amount.

The National Recovery and Resilience Plan (NRRP), drafted by the Italian government and approved by the European Commission, is the document that the Italian government has drawn up to illustrate to the European Commission how the country intends to invest the funds that will be provided in the framework of the Next Generation EU initiative.

The document describes the projects that Italy intends to deliver with the help of the EU funds. The plan also outlines how these resources will be managed and presents a roadmap for related reforms, which are aimed partly at implementing the plan and partly at modernising the country.

The plan was written according to the European Commission's official guidelines and is structured around three main axes: digitalisation and innovation, environmental transition, and social inclusion. The NRRP groups its investment projects into 16 components, which are in turn classified under 6 mission headings: Digitalisation, innovation, competitiveness, culture and tourism; Green revolution and environmental transition; Infrastructure for sustainable mobility; Education and research; Cohesion and inclusion; Healthcare.

According to a report published by the Italian Parliament's Research Centre, the government estimates the impact of the NRRP on the country's economy to be a growth of 0.8%, bringing the potential growth rate in the final year of the plan up to 1.4%.

Alongside the investment projects, the NRRP also outlines the reforms that the government intends to adopt in an effort to modernise the country. The plan distinguishes between four different families of reforms: horizontal or contextual: measures in the public interest; enabling: interventions serving to guarantee the implementation of the plan; sectoral: related to individual missions or, in any case, to specific areas; contributive: not strictly related to the implementation of the plan, but nevertheless necessary for the modernisation of the country (such as the reform of the tax system or of social safety nets).

Finally, the management of the NRRP has been laid out by a specific implementation Decree. All actors involved in the plan (including ministries and other administrations, both central and local) will be called upon to implement the measures and reforms that fall within their remit. A coordination facility will be established at the Ministry of Economy and Finance to monitor and oversee its implementation, as well as to liaise with the European Commission. Under the control of the Prime Minister, meanwhile, a steering committee will be set up in order to monitor the progress of the plan, as well as to propose the activation of any substitutive powers that may be necessary and the regulatory changes required to implement the plan.

As previously mentioned, Italy is the main beneficiary of this new EU funding programme, with €191.5 billion of funds provided, split between grants (€68.9 billion) and loans (€122.6 billion). In addition to these resources, the country will also benefit from approximately €13 billion under the Recovery Assistance for Cohesion and the Territories of Europe (REACT-EU) programme. The government has also allocated a further €30.62 billion for the completion of the projects contained in the NRRP.

The lion's share of the resources has been earmarked for the implementation of the projects that fall under mission heading 2 of the plan (green revolution and environmental transition), which will receive just under €60 billion. Mission 1 (digitalisation, innovation, competitiveness, culture and tourism) has been allocated some

€40.7 billion, whilst mission 4 (education and research) will see almost €31 billion. Around €25 billion will then be dedicated to sustainable infrastructure, roughly €20 billion for cohesion and inclusion, and approximately €15 billion for healthcare.

However, these are not the only resources available for actions intended to combat the effects of the pandemic and kickstart Italy's recovery. Indeed, the EU is making over €330 billion available for regional and local projects in the period spanning 2021–2027 through its structural funds, in an effort to help reduce economic disparities and aid recovery from the pandemic. The Cohesion Package 2021–2027 involves multi-annual investments, with most of the resources going to the least developed countries and regions so as to promote social, economic and territorial cohesion throughout the EU. In the current situation of crisis, in addition to mitigating the long-term social and economic effects of the pandemic, this will also help to grease the wheels of the single market. In this context, Italy will be able to count on a further €50 billion through the complex mechanism of Eu programming.

The planning of the Structural Funds 2021–2027 is based around five new strategic objectives, each reflecting the EU's main priorities: a smarter, more competitive Europe; a greener, more resilient, lower-carbon Europe transitioning towards a net-zero-carbon economy; a more connected Europe; a Europe made more social and inclusive through the implementation of the European Pillar of Social Rights; a Europe that is closer to its citizens.

This picture—both general and partial—of the resources to be made available to European countries, and to Italy in particular, for structural investments over the coming years undoubtedly represents an exceptionally complex challenge for all levels of vertical governance. For one thing, there is the need to use these resources efficiently, within a very tight timeframe, and according to strict reporting rules. For another, there is a clear risk that the administrations responsible will not be able to manage these resources effectively, in a way that would coordinate the actions of the different funds and build projects capable of integrating different objectives.

If we look at policies for cities in particular, it becomes clear that the enormous amount of resources that will have to be managed in urban areas risks being fragmented into a vast range of uncoordinated operations, entirely overlooking any logic of an integrated and strategic nature.

This prospect becomes all the more serious when we consider that post-pandemic economic growth in Italy is likely to have a significantly urban focus (Viesti 2021), with the development of advanced tertiary sectors that are heavily concentrated in urban areas and the much-hoped-for recovery of the tertiary sectors most severely affected by the pandemic (tourism, commerce, culture).

That said, as we have already explored, some of the most deep-seated inequalities are to be found in cities—particularly generational and gender, as well as those related to the foreign population—and these are only growing. From this perspective, the projects promoted within the framework of the EU's planning should be able to forge new job opportunities for young people—especially foreigners—and for women, in order to compensate for the many doors that have closed, including by improving the territorial services that can encourage and support working women in particular, such as by reducing their caring responsibilities. Inequalities between generations, between the genders and between Italians and foreigners can primarily be seen in the growing duality of the labour market, between stable jobs and widespread precarity. This is more evident in cities, where there is the most intense concentration of not only the more highly skilled service sector, but also that of the lower-value-added services.

On the other hand, both green and digital transformation can find opportunities for development and experimentation in urban areas, for example in the use of data and connectivity for mobility, or for the dimensioning of territorial services.

As already seen in previous chapters, urban areas will be the most severely affected by the changes due to the pandemic, the evolutionary beginnings of which can be already glimpsed (remote working, structural growth of online shopping and delivery services, transformations of the housing market) and the actual extent of which when fully complete cannot yet be predicted (which/how many changes are temporary and which/how many will become structural), but for which we need to have public policies ready and waiting.

NRRP and programming of the Structural Funds should therefore be considered a tool for establishing the sorts of projects and policies capable of reducing the inequalities between and within cities.

In this sense, if the fifth mission of NRRP (Social, gender and territorial equality) is directly geared towards achieving this objective, all the other missions—and in particular those relating to the green transition, mobility infrastructure, and education, training, research and culture, but also digitalisation and healthcare—play an essential role in pursuing three goals:

- establishing specific priority actions for the most fragile areas of urban contexts (peripheral neighbourhoods both with and without public housing, urban areas characterised by situations of environmental and territorial risk, but also parts of the historical centre suffering from depopulation), concentrating resources on these areas and paying attention to their capacity to produce new (and high-quality) jobs;
- integrating tangible and intangible actions, building on the foundation of public assets (schools, social, healthcare and welfare services, sports and leisure facilities, parks and open spaces) to create integrated projects with the capacity to involve local resources and different administrational sectors;
- adopting the environmental crisis as an essential filter for projects and policies, leaning towards urban and environmental conversion processes with very clear-cut choices (less large infrastructure, more maintenance and upgrading in terms of energy consumption and environment; zero land consumption; improving energy efficiency not only for owner-occupied houses, but also for rented ones, encouraging a rebalancing towards the latter; strong investment in sustainable cycling and pedestrian mobility, including with a view to commuter mobility needs).

How can we pursue these ambitious goals, from the point of view of governance mechanisms? How can we build integrated projects that are able to promote territorial projects in cities and bring a variety of different actors, resources and processes together and focused on a single urban context?

This integration would have to be ensured in two ways: first, through the development—in municipalities and perhaps also in metropolitan cities—of very simple spatialised strategic frameworks that identify the challenges, priorities, and particularly fragile target areas. These frameworks could be used by cities as a point of reference for the various sources of funding (NRRP, 2021/2027 planning, other sources), whilst at the same time ensuring coherence between different lines of action. These should not be the ambitious yet often unrealistic strategic plans all too commonly seen; rather, those responsible should produce simple documents that allow for different tangible and intangible actions to be connected with one another for the mutual benefit of different missions and goals. Second, through territorial implementation facilities (at the scale of urban sectors, neighbourhoods, networks of municipalities) capable of managing the complex machinery of application—which will be a colossal task—and providing an up-to-date, uniform framework for monitoring and evaluation. In other words, variable-geometry yet intersectoral implementation units capable of establishing a shared direction and unified management for the many and varied initiatives they oversee.

These are, without a doubt, ambitious objectives, both because of the scarcity of human and cognitive resources in public administrations and because of the prevailing cultures and the intense bureaucratisation of policies so characteristic of the situation in Italy. Not to mention that if current expenditure is not able to cover services that are predominantly or exclusively managed by public operators (transportation, social services), it would not be at all inconceivable for the effects of the new wave of planning in cities to be seen in the costs, but not in the expected results in terms of the actual availability of services.

7.4   An Example: EU Structural Funds Programming in Lombardy

To conclude, I would like to try to present an operational experiment that is still ongoing in order to demonstrate the sorts of processes and mechanisms that can be activated in an attempt to address the difficult challenge of planning out the use of EU resources in the post-pandemic period.

Specifically, this is a project supporting the start of the planning of the structural funds—in particular the ERDF and ESF for the 2021–2027 period—initiated in the Lombardy region. The involvement of my department, which began in early 2020, led to a collaboration agreement between the DAStU and the regional government's Structural Funds Planning Office in the context of planning integrated policies for urban development.

The logic guiding this experiment was that of framing planning as a shared co-design process between the Region and the individual municipalities, in which establishing the content of the regional operational programmes was the result of a planning activity put forward by the municipalities on the issue of territorial cohesion within cities, with reference to the effects of social fragilization due in part to the pandemic.

The first move involved the promotion of an Expression of Interest, open to all municipalities in Lombardy that are provincial capitals or with over 50,000 inhabitants (a total of 18 municipalities), in which the regional government asked the municipalities to develop a preliminary strategy for tackling the issue of inequality in urban areas, supporting the implementation of specific sustainable urban development strategies.

In terms of content, this preliminary strategy had to offer an interpretation of the problems of an urban area with the overall goal of regenerating certain areas by leveraging the dimension of housing, education, and the quality of social and healthcare services, aiming to increase the social inclusion of the most fragile segments of the population (in terms of age and material and immaterial poverty) and to reduce material and immaterial inequalities by focusing action on local communities.

The premise of the expression of interest was that the target areas selected by the municipal governments had to be amongst those in which the inequalities and fragilities already present had been further exacerbated by the direct and indirect effects of the COVID-19 pandemic, which brought to light their true significance and extent. This worsening of conditions of deprivation manifested itself over the course of 2020 in various forms, connected to the disparities in terms of the size, quality and comfort of domestic space; the technological gap owing to the limitations on internet connectivity and a lack of sufficient technological devices, which primarily, though not exclusively, affected school-age children; the reduction or even disappearance of sources of income, especially for families and individuals in precarious working conditions and employed in sectors particularly severely affected by the lockdown; and difficulty accessing territorial services, which are often less structured than in other areas of cities.

On the other hand, in the fragile contexts of urban areas, even during the most arduous months of the pandemic, it was common to see communities, associations and private social groups mobilising intensely—often with the support of public administrations—in their efforts to assist individuals, families and social groups in particularly difficult situations.

To address at least some of the factors responsible for producing and reproducing these inequalities, the municipalities were asked to develop a long-term, non-episodic strategy that was both adequately funded and capable of acting on various levers, namely employment, social and environmental fronts.

The municipalities to which the expression of interest was addressed were then called upon to propose an integrated, localised project set within the framework of a unified urban strategy, built around priority themes or lines of action.

The first of these themes is the improvement of housing services (upgrading buildings) in tandem with the improvement of the urban environment (upgrading public spaces) and strengthening the ties of social cohesion and the local community. Measures taken against the fragility of housing can involve both tangible and intangible actions, promote social inclusion, partly through the definition of employment and training policies, improve environmental efficiency and combat energy poverty, rethink and redesign open and public spaces, including with a view to over-hauling the forms and practices of proximity, strengthen community networks, and improve the engagement of associations and private social groups (including through the voluntary sector).

The second priority line of action is focused on bolstering education, for all age groups, by reorganising educational spaces, upgrading schools and establishing cutting-edge workshops, fostering the links between schools and territories, and improving teacher training. The idea suggested by this second area of intervention is to reimagine schools as community hubs, potentially even opening beyond normal school hours, with projects dedicated to the community (school of the third age, libraries and study spaces, theatres and gyms). A further key point of this is that schools should be considered and designed in close relation to the space around them, and as such, the projects could reconfigure their surrounding areas (school squares and streets as protected areas for children's play and leisure activities, including extracurricular activities). In this context, it is essential to create and consolidate networks between school and society (even through projects with the voluntary sector, including for the most vulnerable students) and between school and work (through collaborative projects with the world of work and a review of how vocational training schemes are managed).

The third priority theme to be addressed is focused on promoting the territorial social and healthcare service, as well as social welfare services, by strengthening the local medical and welfare community, improving the spaces and facilities available (by upgrading the buildings which the services of the Local Healthcare and Welfare Authorities—ASSTs operate out of, developing the level of digitalisation, etc.); creating short, integrated networks between services and their uses, favouring the provision of home care over residential care (by experimenting with urban versions of Territorial Healthcare and Welfare Facilities, involving neighbourhood networks in the provision of services and the use of telemedicine, remote monitoring, etc.), making preventative care a priority.

With reference to this third area of intervention, the Expression of Interest suggested considering measures/actions aimed at the territorialisation and strength-ening of social and healthcare services in close connection with strategies for the regeneration and reuse of spaces in fragile areas.

As transversal working tools, the Expression of Interest focused on the connec-tivity of local communities through the centrality of tangible and intangible digital technologies, as well as the promotion of local social capital and the voluntary sector as networks for cohesion.

The area of intervention selected (neighbourhood or urban sector, but also a network of spatially and functionally interconnected areas) had to be justified on the basis of quantitative and qualitative considerations and data.

Finally, the projects proposed had to support the territories and communities that suffered the most intense socio-economic effects of the pandemic. As such, the projects were required to work towards the social inclusion of the most fragile urban populations, on whom the pandemic has had the greatest impact, partly because of inequalities in income, knowledge and skills; elderly people, women, children and young people, the most fragile social groups from a socio-economic perspective.

The municipalities were asked to develop two lines of reasoning. First, the definition of a strategic frame of reference on an urban scale, allowing them to identify the strategic challenges involved in achieving social cohesion and innovation objectives as well as providing arguments for the definition of the context(s) in which they wished to launch an integrated project for sustainable urban development and regeneration. Second, the initial identification of objectives and tools for the design of an integrated project, along with the initial identification of flagship measures and actions to be rolled out in their selected urban area. These measures/actions, which must be clearly integrated into the strategy, must be of a high standard and replicable, showcasing the qualities of the local system as a whole. The projects should also seek to improve the activities of the public administration and its ability to forge networks in local communities.

The publication of the Expression of Interest was prepared by way of open meetings with the eligible municipalities and the drafting of working tools for administrations, including an Open Book drawn up by the DAStU (DAStU, Regione Lombardia 2021), ultimately leading to the submission of 16 preliminary strategies, 12 of which were recommended for funding in March 2021. The recommendation specifies funding of €15 million for each municipality, to be taken from the ERDF and the ESF resources programmed through Regional Operative Programmes.

Following the selection of the strategies to be funded, an intensive co-planning process was launched in conjunction with the municipalities—which is still ongoing as of July 2021—leading to the revision of the strategies and the presentation of technical and operational data sheets for the implementation of the integrated tangible and intangible actions involved.

Meanwhile, the ERDF and ESF Regional Operational Programmes based on the strategies and actions proposed by the municipalities are being drafted and will subsequently have to be approved by the European Commission.

Without venturing to overestimate the value of a project that is ultimately rather limited and highly experimental, I believe that the process initiated by the Lombardy regional government is of interest for a few reasons, both in terms of the content of the strategies and in terms of the process itself.

The preliminary urban development strategy is not intended to be a sectoral strategy, but rather a frame of reference for the problems and opportunities involved in sustainable urban development, which is also linked to this somewhat shaky phase of the life of Lombardy's municipalities.

The delimitation of the area for intervention has been established as the result of a strategic reflection and can be centred on a fragile residential area (a neighbourhood or urban district, for example), but equally on a system of school complexes or a network of healthcare and welfare services located in areas of the city affected by particular critical issues, be they on the peripheries or in more central areas.

The urban development strategy should be the result of an effort to integrate issues and skills, whilst the implementation phase should be managed by intersectoral implementation units. Moreover, the projects undertaken should build effective partnerships that are geared towards producing concrete, feasible results based on the proposals submitted. The dimension of involving stakeholders and residents is not only for the purpose of building consensus, but also for qualifying the projects and making them more effective.

Schools as well as healthcare and welfare services are held to be essential pieces of the puzzle when crafting social inclusion strategies at the community level and strategies for the material improvement of areas characterised by situations of social hardship and material deterioration.

These innovative elements—as we have seen by working very closely with the regional and municipal governments—require an exceptional amount of effort from the administrations involved. Indeed, an approach of this kind with a focus on effectiveness over efficiency has to deal with the rules and mechanisms of expenditure, with administrations often lacking sufficient resources to manage complex projects, and with a dearth of experience in thinking in terms of the unitary, intersectoral management of interventions.

Essentially, we realised that even a limited experiment such as the one undertaken by the Lombardy regional government requires a transformation in its forms of reason which, in my view, constitutes a prerequisite for the effectiveness of all the investments to be planned for urban areas over the coming years.

From this perspective, an antifragile approach to planning is one which resists the urge to rush things, one which embraces the highly uncertain nature of the context, one which works on improving the abilities of the actors involved, one which embraces the possibility of accidents, forks in the road and surprises, one which integrates different administrative rationales and cultures by considering the territory not as a mere backdrop, but as a fundamental operator in public action.

References

Balducci A, Chiffi D, Curci F (eds.) (2020) Risk and resilience. Socio-spatial and environmental challenges. Springer Brief, Berlin-Milano
Blečić I, Cecchini A (2016) Verso una pianificazione antifragile. Come pensare al futuro senza prevederlo. Franco Angeli, Milano
Cersosimo D, Donzelli C (eds) (2020) Manifesto per riabitare l'Italia. Donzelli, Roma
Chiffi D, Curci F (2019) Fragility: concept and related notions. Territorio 91:55–59
DAStU, Regione Lombardia (2021) Open Book. Casi ed esperienze. Milano
Deleuze G (1990) Expressionism in philosophy: Spinoza. Zone Books, New York
Infussi F (2019) Fragilità primer. Territorio 91:60–63
Lanzani A (2020) Fragilità territoriali. In Cersosimo D, Donzelli C (ed) Manifesto per riabitare l'Italia. Donzelli, Roma p 121–128
Taleb NN (2012a) Antifragile: things that gain from disorder. Random House, New York
Taleb NN (2012b) The Black Swan. The impact of highly improbable. Random House, New York
Thom R (1989) Structural stability and morphogenesis: an outline of a general theory of models. Addison-Wesley, Reading (MA)
UNDDR (2020) The human cost of disasters 2000–2019. UN Office for Disaster Risk Reduction, New York
Viesti G (2021) Centri e periferie. Laterza, Bari

Conclusions: Usable Knowledge

Abstract The conclusions try to reflect on the role of discourses and expert knowledge in the definition of effective strategies for post-pandemic cities. The hypothesis presented in these conclusions is that planning and design expertise can play a crucial role in defining post-pandemic urban strategies if they will be able to produce "usable knowledge" and to contribute, in a transdisciplinary dialogue, to redefine urban agendas and narratives.

Since the very first and most severe lockdown, we have been hit by an incredible number of discourses. Common discourse, scientific discourse, political discourse. These discourses, these endless discussions, and debates, have been to do with the medical dimension of the pandemic —its dramatic effects on health, its dynamics, its epidemiological spread—but also its causes, its relationships with other phenomena (political, environmental and psychological, to name but a few). The words of experts have literally invaded our lives, our television and computer screens, our newspapers and magazines, our social networks.

I am not knowledgeable enough to perform an analysis of these discourses, of their contradictions, of the changes in direction of experts who apodictically proclaim scientific truths, only to disprove them a few days later, of the arguments between virologists and epidemiologists in TV studios, of the thousands of hours of broadcasts jam-packed with operational instructions on how to contain the epidemic and limit its effects on our daily lives.

I would, however, like to stress that any such analysis should be carried out carefully. First of all, we should ask ourselves what principles of legitimacy and authority have characterised these often contradictory and certainly ever-changing assertions. Indeed, the arena in which these experts have delivered their pronouncements—influencing not only our lives, but also political decisions—has not (at least for the most part) been that of scientific discussion between peers, but that of the public sphere and common discourse. This means that the mechanisms by which these discourses, their influence and their effectiveness have been legitimised has not depended in the slightest on the systems for scrutiny and verification belonging to the field of scientific research, but rather on other processes of accreditation characteristic of the public sphere.

G. Pasqui, *Coping with the Pandemic in Fragile Cities*, PoliMI SpringerBriefs,
https://doi.org/10.1007/978-3-030-93979-3

Secondly, we should be able to follow the thread of the "invisible power", to borrow an expression from Sini (2013), that pervades these discourses unbeknownst to them, compromising their supposed neutrality and scientific nature whilst also casting light on how and to what extent each and every scientific claim is caught up in a wider tangled web of powers and knowledge, in which economic and geopolitical interests—but also worldviews and contexts of meaning—play an essential role. Throughout the pandemic, the discourse delivered by experts has never been pure in nature.

Finally, we should try to understand the effectiveness of these discourses, their subsumption into other practices, both discursive and otherwise, their influence on collective decisions and individual lives, the way in which the words of expert knowledge have been re-assimilated and reassembled into other practices of power and knowledge.

All this has nothing to do with the tone-deaf return of anti-scientific ideas, which shrilly proclaim the existence of conspiracies and reject the results of scientific research. An exploration of the ways in which science has been used during the pandemic (both in scientific discourse and in common discourse based on some supposed scientific objectivity) would undoubtedly make for a case study of exceptional interest. On the one hand, we have seen the salvific power of science and technology come to fruition. Without the Internet, which allowed resuscitators on the front lines in hospitals in the four corners of the world to share their information and experiences in real time, without big data and the computing power that has grown enormously in recent decades, without the capability of drawing upon extraordinarily effective experimental protocols, we would not even have a vaccine today, nor would we have the medications that are keeping the number of deaths at a minimum. On the other hand, we can hardly contain our dismay at just how irresponsible the claims and affirmations of scientists have been (broadcast everywhere, on social media as well as on television), given that over the past year, they have preached everything under the sun, as well as the opposite—in speeches which have, by the by, been used for political and business purposes in more than one unspeakable case.

This way of considering the role and pervasiveness of expert knowledge during the pandemic also applies to the discourses fabricated about the city, churned out by any number of architects, urban planners, sociologists and anthropologists, but also by everyone who observed the connections between the transformations of urban space and the pandemic.

I have already remarked upon how the dominant emotional tones in the field of architecture and urban studies have oscillated between two extremes: an apocalyptic emotional tone—which has even gone so far as to predict even the end of the city itself and a gradual rearticulation of settlement models on a global scale—and a point of view oriented towards the pressing need to reconstruct tools to take us back to our previous state, in an attempt to exorcise the disruptive nature of the pandemic and its impacts.

In this context, and at the conclusion of this small volume, I would instead like to reflect upon the possible use of these discourses on urban space as a means of crafting a new wave of policies for the city, highlighting how even when it comes to our knowledge and discursive practices, it is necessary for us to reflect carefully on the possibilities of use (rather than on utility).

A volume published in Italy in 2021 and entitled *How cities and territories will change after Covid-19. The theses of ten urban planners* (Nigrelli 2021), allows us to think precisely about the way in which urban planning should rethink its way of thinking after the pandemic. In his contribution Stefano Munarin writes for example.

> Today, if we are interested in addressing the territorial events connected with this pandemic, we must resume a new long journey of formation; understand which are the "new knowledge" with which to dialogue, which other inter / trans disciplinary relationships we must activate (Munarin 2021: 136)

It is therefore not just a question of reviewing the operational tools of urban planning, but also of thinking about the possible uses of our knowledge between the long time of the city and the fleetingness of the news. To do this, it is essential to understand that the cities hit by the wave of COVID require a new work agenda.

I do not think it is yet the time for certainties, for the design of defined scenarios, for projections that are too sure. It seems to me that we can be content with setting up a well-organized work agenda, which can help us reorient programs and projects, define new ones, build effective work platforms.

This can be done starting from a fundamental assumption: it is important to confirm, deepen, develop those themes and research programs that already grasped the dimension of the fragility of the territories and that engage policies, projects and public action. In other words, we must first put our skills to work in rethinking and reorienting what we are already doing.

Furthermore, it is essential to understand how to identify the skills that could be put at the service of the institutions and that could be useful to put a spatial and territorial perspective on the agenda at national, regional and local level today almost absent from public discussion and policy orientations.

First of all, it is a question of highlighting some background themes, which seem decisive to us for understanding the "sense of the whole" of the dramatic situation we are in and its possible outcomes.

The Return of the Public and the Role of Design Disciplines and Urban Studies

The crisis of a model of global capitalism that is unable to insure and reinsure risk (pandemics, climate change) puts the question of the public, the role and meaning of public action at the center of attention once again. regulation, in the government and in the project of the city, the territory and the landscape. In this context, policies on a regional, national and European scale will necessarily mobilize important public investments and will require a massive effort of planning and implementation imagination. The skills of the city's planners and scholars ask us to carefully reflect on the role of the territorialization of investments, which has also proved to be one of the major weaknesses in the expansion phase of the epidemic. What role can our knowledge play in directing and guiding probable (and desirable) public investments? How can we rethink our academic role at this juncture?

The Disputed City and the Skills Crisis: The Relationship with Other Knowledge

The pandemic shows the difficulty of integrating different knowledge and to connect skills and political decisions. What new relationships (and conflicts) with other knowledge will this and other similar environmental and health emergencies entail? Who should we learn to listen, with whom should we learn to dialogue? What new covenants do we need to learn to cultivate? How can the skills of spatial planners be really useful in the planning and design phase of the interventions that have been implemented by the European Union and by the national states?

Daily Life and Forms of Control

The pandemic has activated a variety of forms, some unprecedented, of social control through spatial control. In democratic regimes, it is a question of extreme delicacy, which has a very strong spatial value. How to deal with the question of forms of control: borders and confinements, geographical dimension of containment interventions, remote control? What cautions and concerns for the prospects of democracy and citizenship?

Urban Practices, Living Practices

Forms of living, places of sharing, public space have been and will certainly be affected by the consequences of the pandemic, in Italy and in the world. What will be the possible effects of the pandemic on urban space use practices? What to think of the sharing dimension? What effects on possible phenomena of "introversion" of life practices? What new meaning and role for the dimension of interior spaces?

At the source of these background problems it is possible to identify a research agenda that allows to enhance the skills of architecture, urban planning and urban studies.

Urban Spaces, in the Short Term

The new urban agendas should be able to work on how to contribute to the cognitive and informative framework with respect to mapping of cases and criticalities that link epidemic / contagion / places and spatial organization of urban activities. How to use local contexts (for example neighborhoods) to test needs and agendas for short-term public action (mobility, local services, reorganization of workplaces)?

Resilience, Economy and Fundamental Services: How Territories Can Prepare Themselves

A central theme is that of public services, fundamental economic activities and material welfare as resilient infrastructures. How do we think and imagine it is necessary to reorganize the activities of the fundamental economy, services and territorial equipment starting from the health and social-health facilities and their territorial organization? How to work on the territorial dimension of basic services (school, training, networks, material welfare)? What infrastructure for prepared territories, to cope with the heavy repercussions on the economies of entire territories, the worsening of poverty and the problematic rearticulation of social relations? How to deal with extremely urgent issues such as the design and management of residences and services for the elderly?

The Social Dimension: Elderly and Frail People, Migrants

The elderly and frail were those most directly and indirectly affected by the pandemic. It is a decisive node, which brings into play the territorial forms of the organization of regional health systems, the logic of specialization and centralization based on excellence, but also the role of volunteering and the third sector. How to ensure the strengthening of the territorial policies of active surveillance and social and health care of chronic and fragile users? How to think of a regional health system that is more focused on prevention than treatment? These issues also have a strong planning, as well as management and policy value. A further theme concerns policies for migrants, legal or otherwise, who will be among the subjects most exposed to the economic and social effects of the crisis.

Schools, as a Fundamental Safeguard: Connectivity and Relationship With Families

All school age groups, considering the age differences in any case, have suffered a very strong impact on the continuity of school activities and on socialization opportunities. Schools and families had to reorganize quickly after the closure of the school complexes and with the cancellation of the activities in the presence. Schools reacted to the situation voluntarily and according to the digital skills of teachers and school leaders. Not all schools and not all teachers have been able to react quickly to the situation with obvious delays in the activation of forms of distance learning. On the side of students and families, the variable was once again the presence of IT equipment and digital skills. A reflection on schools, especially in fragile contexts such as urban suburbs, and on the need for integrated projects of a territorial nature that hinge on schools is therefore decisive.

Forms of the Territory, Settlement Patterns and Pandemics

Without forcing hasty interpretations, the spread of the virus throughout the national territory has on the one hand brought back to the foreground, made manifest, the articulation of the Italian settlement system: small towns, densely inhabited valleys, compact centers, large cities, dispersed and scattered settlements, etc. (Trigilia and Burroni 2009; Balducci et al. 2017; Lanzani et al. 2020; Viesti 2021); and it leads to reflection on possible future processes, on the effects of this emergency (and consequent economic crisis) on the distribution of the population and production (Florida et al. 2021). How did the virus spread, what different situations can we recognize (in relation to settlement systems but also socio-health)? And what thrusts will all this produce in future settlement processes? How to imagine the rearticulation of Italian territories in the post-virus: are we moving towards new equilibrium between metropolitan Italy, middle Italy and inland areas?

Policies, Programs and Investments After the Epidemic

The occasion of public investments and a new season of programming asks us to reflect on the priorities, including territorial ones, of current policies and programs. How can we think of the phase that opens up to us as a place for experimenting with a great project for the ecological reconversion of cities and territories? How to integrate the issues raised by the emergency with other major environmental issues, which cannot be forgotten or postponed? Can a national maintenance program for fragile territories make an important contribution to the recovery of our country?

The implementation of this agenda needs a reflection on design techniques and tools. What effects will the epidemic have on the forms and contents of our design tools? How to set up a reflection on the forms and devices of the project? How to deal with the urban market and its possible dynamics in plans and projects? Through which processes and tools can the knowledge of the project contribute to the country?

This is a partial agenda, which however shows how fundamental a strongly self-reflective attitude on the part of the cultures of planning and urban design.

In a very interesting text, Cristina Bianchetti, Camillo Boano and Antonio Di Campli critically reflect on what they have dubbed "quarantine urbanism" (Bianchetti et al. 2020). Amongst other musings, they write:

> Reintroducing the centrality of the urban issue means placing the shattered, disjointed character of vulnerability firmly back at the centre; the ethical connotation of the link between the body and space; rethinking places outside of the usual conservative shortcuts; the need for new infrastructures for care that are bold enough to retread old paths in a different way. All this requires an approach to planning that is not defensive, but rather affirmative. The pandemic requires us to emerge from the political economy of mourning, melancholy and reconstruction. Is it possible to imagine affirmative design practices, capable of responding to horizons of hope and resistance that do not consign us to nihilism? We may not know, but we seem to sense that this means that it is not useful to refer to yet another urbanism - to one of the many clichés that have cropped up in the impetuous, and at times disjointed, public debate seen in recent weeks (Bianchetti et al. 2020: 9).

Although I may not subscribe to all the steps in the authors' thought process here, I take this text as an injunction to an ethics of discourse and a politics of knowledge. An ethics of discourse understood as self-reflexive attention to the world in which what we say and write is subsumed into other political and symbolic practices. A politics of knowledge understood as suspicion of any discourse that presents itself as predicative and self-evident, based a legitimising force that is often rooted in different rationales.

Contemplating the post-pandemic city, as I have sought to do in this book, therefore means testing out different hypotheses, contending with the tangled knot of knowledge and power that characterises the public scene, rooting every reflection and proposal in an attentive observation of everyday life, but also contending with the given material, political and institutional conditions, and experimenting with the realms of possibility without ever losing sight of the limits of our own knowledge in action.

Architecture, urban planning and urban studies can certainly play a central role in the public debate on the future of cities, provided that they are capable to deal with some difficult issues, first and foremost rebuilding an approach to planning and public action that is up to the challenge of dealing with radical uncertainty—one that is both visionary and highly pragmatic (Perulli 2021). Offering concrete solutions here and now, without giving up on the prospect of thinking in a different way about the city, about bodies and their relationships, but also about the ways in which our discourse on the city is transformed into policies, plans, investments.

Finally, I propose to consider the pandemic as a symptom of a broader urban crisis—one which we can only conceivably address by politicising the matter of the ecological transition and embracing the centrality of the issue of growing socio-spatial inequalities and injustices as fundamental avenues for a renewed conception of public action to explore.

References

Balducci A, Fedeli V, Curci F (eds) (2017) Post-metropolitan territories: looking for a new urbanity. Routledge, London

Bianchetti C (2021) Bodies: between space and design. Jovis, Barcelona

Bianchetti C, Boano C, Di Campli A (2020) Against Quarantine Urbanism. Che cosa può, se può, il progetto? Territorio 92:7–9

Florida R, Rodríguez-Pose A, Storper M (2021) Cities in a post-Covid World. Urban Studies. First published online June 27, 2021.

Lanzani A, De Leo D, Mattioli C, Zanfi E (2020) Nell'Italia di mezzo: rigenerazione e valorizzazione dei territori della produzione. Coppola A, Del Fabbro M, Lanzani A, Pessina G, Zanfi F (a cura di) Ricomporre i divari. Politiche e progetti territoriali contro le disuguaglianze e per la transizione ecologica. Il Mulino, Bologna, pp 107–116

Munarin S (2021) La pandemia contesa. Riflessioni tra il tempo lungo della città e la fugacità della cronaca ai tempi del coronavirus. In Nigrelli F C (ed.) Come cambieranno le città e i territori dopo il Covid-19. Le tesi di dieci urbanisti, Quodlibet Studio, Macerata, p 125–138

Nigrelli F C (ed.) Come cambieranno le città e i territori dopo il Covid-19. Le tesi di dieci urbanisti, Quodlibet Studio, Macerata

Perulli P (2021) Nel 2050. Passaggio al nuovo mondo. Il Mulino, Bologna

Sini C (2013) Inizio. Jaca Book, Milano

Triglia C, Burroni L (2009) Italy: rise, decline and restructuring of a regionalized capitalism. Econ Soc 38(4):630–653

Viesti G (2021) Centri e periferie. Laterza, Bari